What they're saying about H
Management and The Synerg

"We have had tremendous success with Holt Marketing. Our return on investment for marketing is over 99% and growing fast. We wouldn't be anywhere without Holt. Holt Marketing & Management makes it very difficult not to excel."

Jonathan Laundra -
President Internal Operations
J.D. Laundra Foundations & Masonry

"An excellent and concise resource that explains how to build unlimited profits in any small business using essential synergy factors."

Dr. B.J. Chang -
Owner
General Scientific Corporation

"Gary Holt is a master at merging common sense with professional business systems."

Greg Laube-
Owner
The Paint Bull, Color Tec and The Finish Zone

"We have been working with Gary Holt and Holt Marketing & Management for the past two years. We have benefited dramatically from the advice of Gary Holt and his training ... Because of this training we have implemented strong management, training, quality control, and operational systems. The use of these systems and training have assisted in the growth of our company and the retention of employees."
Mark R. Artinian -
President and Owner
Bosco's Pizza Company

"The best book I have ever read that describes the true benefits of systems management and business team building into a winning formula for financial freedom. Mr. Holt's ideas and clear explanations make this a must read for every small business owner."
Gary Richards -
Owner
300 Management

"Gary has a knack for keeping us focused on our vision. We never truly understood the process of creating a turn-key business and the incredible freedom that we can create for ourselves until we started working with Gary. Gary has a unique perspective as an outsider to our business and does

not allow us to get bogged down in politics but helps us focus on tangible and intangible results so we can make good business decisions. Don't just go through the motions with Gary, he will see right through you. If you aren't true to your convictions this consultant might just fire you!"
Brian Stadler
Vice President
Wolgast Corporation

"As a company we had reached a plateau without the wisdom to proceed to the next level. With the help of Gary Holt we have gained the management and marketing knowledge to raise us to the next level and beyond. If you want a diploma for your office wall go to college, if you want to learn how to run a successful business talk to Gary Holt. 80% of second-generation businesses fail, with the management and marketing knowledge we have gained from Gary Holt we are prepared to take our company into the second-generation with confidence."
Doug Rechsteiner -
President
Computer Operated Manufacturing, Inc.

"Gary Holt has been my coach for the better part of the past two years. Not only do we have similar philosophies, but Gary offers insight and unique ways of approaching delicate/complex situations. He has been a tremendous help in the growth of my business."

Bill Hogan -
CEO, Hogan Leadership

"A combination of the right people and the right processes orchestrated by good strategy will propel your company's performance. If you want to elevate the performance of your company to the top of its market Gary Holt can help. Put The Synergy Factor to work!"

Mark Pumford -
President
Pumford Construction

The Synergy Factor
The Power of People and Processes to Build Unlimited Profits in Any Business
by Gary Holt

ORCHESTRATION
PUBLICATION

To Linda
My wife, the love of my life,
my soul mate

To my sons; Keith, Kevin, and Steven
My wish is for your business to
give you more of what you need
and want

The Synergy Factor: The Power of People and Processes to Build Unlimited Profits in any Business
Copyright © 2001 by Holt Marketing & Management Services
All rights reserved, including the right of reproduction in whole or in part in any form
Cover design by Paul Kowalski
Published by Orchestration Publication

Manufactured in the United States of America
10 9 8 7 6 5 4 3 2 1
ISBN: 0-9708844-0-0

Acknowledgements

I'd like to take this opportunity to thank those people whose help, patience, and encouragement made this book possible.

To my wife and partner, Linda Holt, for her support, tirelessness, excellent proofreading and language skills. She helped me get it right.

To Lin Ponn, my assistant for 10 years, for typesetting thousands of pages of material and always encouraging me by pointing out the value of my efforts.

To Dawn Josephson of Cameo Publications for her editorial excellence in organizing my work.

To Paul Kowalski for creating the book's cover. His creative insight and expertise are appreciated.

Last, but not least, I'd like to thank you, our incredible clients and friends, for your business and trust. Together we will make the next few years the best ever!

Table of Contents

Part I 1

Introduction 1
The Origin of The Synergy Factor 1
In the Beginning 3
The Unlimited Power of The Synergy Factor 7
The Right People 10
What is a Process? 12

Chapter One 18
The First Step to High Performance 18
Process Driven Teams are The Key 23

Chapter Two 26
Why 96% of all Businesses Eventually Fail 26
Plan for Smarter Choices 35
What Owners and Managers Do: Illusion versus Reality 39
Position Functions 40
Make the Time for Success 41

Part II 44

Chapter Three 44

The First Synergy Factor 44
The Leadership & Management Team: The Keys to Happy and Productive Employees 44
Productivity Strategy 47
The Difference Between Leadership and Management 54
The Leadership and Management Synergy Factor Will Keep Your Doors Open 56

The Leadership and Management Synergy Factor Works............59

Chapter Four 62

The Second Synergy Factor 62
The Sales and Marketing Team – The Lifeblood of Your
Business 62
Marketing versus Sales..63
Branding is a Vital Component..64
The Sales Synergy 66
The Selling Synergy That Can Increase Your Income Over 200%
in Less than 12 Months..70

Chapter Five 83

The Third Synergy Factor 83
The Operations Team Will Get the Job Done On Time, Every
Time, at a Profit 83
The Restaurant Job Shop 84
Customer Satisfaction..91
What Customer Dissatisfaction and Failed Operations Cost........93

Chapter Six 97

The Fourth Synergy Factor 97
The Finance and Information Team...97
The Lack of The Synergy Factor Can Drain Your Profits..........100
10 Main Reasons for Profit Decline...102
How Financial Synergy Helps Increase Profits..........................103
10 Rules to Increase Profits...105

Chapter Seven 109

The Fifth Synergy Factor 109
Scorecards 109

From Scorecard to Incentives 114
Developing the Game 117

Part III *120*

Chapter Eight **120**

The Biggest Advantage Any Business Can Have is an Educated, Trained Workforce 120
Management Training is Vital As Well 123
How The Synergy Factor Increases Profits and Growth 124
Synergy Factor Training Reduces Cycle Times 126
Synergy Factor Training Increases Employee Motivation 127
Synergy Factor Training Increases Your Company's Velocity .. 128

Chapter Nine **136**

A Typical Business 136
The Gap Analysis 141
The Synergy Factor is Your Process for Success 147

Chapter Ten **149**

Use The Synergy Factor to Ride the Wave to Explosive Cash Flow and Financial Freedom in Any Business **149**

Leadership and Management Team Checklist 151
Marketing, Advertising, and Sales Checklist 153
Operations Checklist 155
Financial Checklist 157
Ride the Wave of The Synergy Factor 159
Where Do We Go From Here? 160
Think Creatively About Your Synergy 165

Conclusion **170**

Afterward **171**

Part I

Introduction

The Origin of The Synergy Factor

It's hard to believe but back in 1985 Holt Marketing and Management Services was a home-based business consisting of my wife and myself. Since then we have grown to provide marketing and advertising services and management training to over 200 companies—positive proof that marketing and management process development and team training work.

The interest for marketing and management process and team development is definitely out there. Smart business owners and managers know that if they are going to grow profitability they need a written plan and trained people working together. Today, businesses are opening in record numbers. That fact alone partly explains the profitable growth of Holt Marketing and Management Services; however, I attribute most of our success to the simple fact that our company solves the number one reason for failure in every business.

What's the reason? Businesses fail primarily because they lack the right people with the right personality for the job and documented processes that all but guarantee success. Let's face it, no business would fail if it had marketing process teams that generated new customers, operating process teams that got everything done on time and on budget, human resource process teams that kept a steady stream of skilled employees on the payroll, and financial process teams that delivered accurate profit and cash flow information to the people every month. This is the essence of the Synergy Factor.

I started this company with the goal of helping small to mid-sized businesses face this challenge head on. I had been successful throughout my entire working career, and I wanted to help others do the same and more—much more. Over the years, I've tried, tested, and perfected many things. Now I want to share my ideas with you to make you a more successful business owner and team leader.

Before we begin, let's back up a few years. Despite the success Holt Marketing and Management Services has today, things weren't always this rosy. As a business owner, I've experienced many of the same challenges you're facing today. Let me tell you my story.

In the Beginning

I accepted a new position as vice president of a small business with sales of approximately $15,000,000 and moved my young family to a new town and a new home. Before we could even get established in our new community, the company sold out, putting me on the street without warning. To add fuel to the fire, the country, and especially our market, was in a severe recession. I found myself with high debts, three hungry teenage boys to feed, and a wife recovering from cancer.

Sure, being at the vice presidential level of any company sounds wonderful, until you discover that the job market for company vice presidents in a small town is zero. In order to support my family, I accepted an executive job with a small company, but it was so poorly run that it was on the verge of bankruptcy and there was little I could do to save it. The next position I accepted was with a family business. At first this seemed promising, but I soon learned that the family members had severe inter-relational problems with each other. Needless to say, this opportunity didn't last long.

I soon came to the conclusion that the only way I could be happy and support my family was to start my own business. I spent months searching for a business opportunity, and after reading my Bible one night I got the courage to commit to investing in a franchise called American Advertising, which was located in Mesa, Arizona.

Unfortunately, the only way I could secure a business loan was by getting a second mortgage on my home. Talk about stress! I had no job, no income, a family to feed, bills to pay, a second mortgage, and no assurance that my new business would succeed. I knew that if I failed, I'd lose everything. I was scared to death.

We were only able to borrow $50,000. Half the money went to pay for the franchise fee, and the other half went into our operating budget. At most I figured we had six months to begin making a profit before the money ran out.

I'll never forget the feeling of 118 degree heat blasting in my face as my wife and I took our first steps off the plane and into the August Arizona heat. We spent two weeks in Mesa, Arizona. Our days consisted of training classes, and our nights were devoted to testing and practicing what we learned during the day. The third week we flew back home and set up our office in our basement.

I spent the fourth week with a successful franchisee in St. Louis, Missouri. He helped me develop my first year operating budget and allowed me to tag along with him and his sales staff to actually see first-hand how the sales and administration part of the business worked.

During the fifth week, an experienced operations manager and trainer came to our office. He spent the week making sure we were following and understanding the operating manual and training us in performing the operations. He had us make sales appointments using the company's processes, so when he arrived we actually made our first sales call.

We suddenly found ourselves working in an industry where we had no experience, doing jobs we had never done before, and selling an unknown product to prospects who had never heard of us or our company. We had no business cards, no brochures, and no previous customers to refer prospects to. But we didn't let that stop us. Within six months our income was greater than what I had made as a vice president of a $35,000,000 company.

Our first employee was our oldest son, and eventually all of our sons joined the company. In less than ten years from our start-up, we achieved our goal of financial independence.

How? I had discovered the secret to small business success, and I learned that secret by observing and working with my own customers, my family, and employees.

Our customers consisted of businesses in every industry. Most of the owners I spoke with did not have an advertising and public relations process. In fact, they had no idea how to develop one. I was more than happy to show them, as this was the scope of our business. After several months of helping them, I began to become friends with many of them. It frustrated me to see them working in their businesses very hard, yet not succeeding like they wanted to.

I watched many of them deal with the same challenges day after day: they couldn't find and retain good people, or they couldn't increase sales, or they couldn't increase profits, or they couldn't increase cash flow. Some were making much less income than I was, even though they had been in business twenty years or more. As I spent time working with these owners and managers, I began to notice for the first time a common theme. Not one of these businesses had the documented processes necessary to make the business work the way it should. What's more, they didn't realize how important it was to have these processes.

These small business owners had no process of measuring the impact each employee had on the quantity, quality, standards, or behavior required to succeed. Since they had none of these vital processes in place, employees were not getting the work done on time. Products lacked the necessary quality. And the company was not making an adequate profit. Additionally, the majority of business owners lacked experience working in a large business and/or in a management position where processes are required.

So this is the secret I discovered: **Synergy.** A business will not grow as profitably year after year without written processes and skilled teams implementing them to create profits.

The Unlimited Power of The Synergy Factor

The Synergy Factor is defined as having the whole be greater than the sum of its parts (talented people + effective processes + profits = synergy).

The Synergy Factor refers to a "team" as being two or more people, joining and working together for the betterment of the company.

As a trainer, I have seen people change, from holding back in the beginning of team process training sessions to totally opening up. As a result of this experience, shared problems are finally realized and new and better processes are created to solve them that no one could have anticipated. The excitement contained in that training session unifies and motivates the team. The people involved in it are empowered by new, fresh thinking and by new and improved alternatives and opportunities.

The results of these interactive sessions can be astounding. Problems that have been around for months, even years, have been solved in a matter of a few hours. A new powerful attitude emerges that says; "We can do it. We can learn together. We can combine our experiences and skills and create better ideas and better ways to create higher performance while allowing us to feel good about it in the process."

People begin to realize that dependent people need others to get what they want. Independent people can get what they want on their own. But interdependent people combine their own efforts with the team to achieve far greater success than could ever be achieved alone. A person must first be independent in order to move ahead to interdependence. It requires even more self-esteem to move to interdependence because to be effective as a team member you can't feel threatened. You can't be defensive.

The two keys to synergy are 1) producing a desired result and 2) the assets that produce that result. Most businesses look at assets as being first financial, such as cash, prepaid expenses, or accounts receivable, or as buildings, equipment, and computers. However, **the most important asset is really people**. It's people that get the results or not. It's people who close the sale, design and make the product, collect the money, pay the bills, and develop the reports to show how we're doing.

The combined knowledge of the industry and people's functional skills leads to ideas for better products, services, and processes. Mentors are developed to support people. Interest in a unified goal creates enthusiasm, building a team that achieves goals with as few resources as possible. They get more with less. The team moves through our rocky environment notching upward and onward. They expand and they create new products and services.

This is The Synergy Factor: Teams creating goals and processes that achieve continuous, predictable, profitable results. It's people being united in a common language, a common goal. It's creative collaboration and cooperation. All of our combined skills, experience, and talent come together to create the miracle of The Synergy Factor.

Back in 1985, first our family members and then our employees, unified in common goals, achieved success by following proven processes that were verified by satisfied clients. We learned these processes from trainers who had successfully done it year after year. Most businesses don't know nor have this synergy, and that's what is preventing them from achieving unlimited profits.

The Right People
In the movie "All The Right Stuff" most of the story line focuses on the tough screening processes NASA uses in selecting the right people to be members of the teams that man America's spacecraft. Maybe you're not going to the moon but you are giving people the responsibility of protecting the most important asset in your life. NASA discovered not just anyone can go to the moon and we have discovered that not just anyone can manage a business. A

manager who does not have leadership in his/her personality cannot take the company to the next level or even keep the company going into the future.

If you are to continue your business long into the future, if you ever want to be free of your business, you must replace yourself with a team that can run the business profitably whether you're there or not. And you must find a leader to lead the team in your absence or your business will not survive. Selecting, assessing, coaching, teaching, terminating managers is the key to unlimited profits in all businesses. Why? Because eventually we're all going to go, so unless you replace yourself with the right people, the profit and the processes necessary for success, your business will fail. Not some times, but *every* time.

Fact #1: If your company does not hire and promote the people that enjoy process and people development and enforce the processes you will not continue to grow as profitably and problem free as you would if you did.

Fact #2: The most difficult thing to do in business is to replace the first owner, while continuing to make profits into the next generation.

Rule #1 - The most important rule; select the right people and develop effective teams

Rule #2 - The business must create a profit and positive cash flow

Rule #3 - You must develop processes that work and train others to implement them

Rule #4 - Your must keep score on every function and person

Rule #5 - You must keep researching for a changing market and change with it, while monitoring your culture and values in the process

What is a Process?

By now you may be wondering what exactly is a process as it relates to business. The most simple definition is this: A process is a collection of tasks or parts that interact as a whole. Processes add value because when combined with people they add synergy, and this is what differentiates a process from a non-process.

The keyword to understanding a process is "interacting." For example, a human is a process. All the parts—the heart, lungs, kidneys, brain, etc.—must work together to be efficient. If someone is chasing you, your brain tells you to run. This causes your heart to speed up and your lungs to process more oxygen. This all happens because of the principle of interaction.

Businesses are no different. If a business lacks leadership processes, it has no exciting goals and the employees aren't motivated. If a business lacks management processes, there is poor organization and poor productivity. If a business lacks marketing processes, it does not have the necessary research and analysis to develop effective advertising and sales processes.

Even if you lack only one of these three processes, it affects the others. For example, if your employees aren't motivated, they'll have no incentive to create high quality products or increase productivity. On the other hand, if your employees are motivated but you have low sales because no marketing and sales processes are in place, they'll eventually lose that motivation because they're worrying about job security, thus causing other parts of the business to break down. Just like the human body, each individual component affects the whole.

Process Mapping

A process map is a visual representation of a process that illustrates:
- Which tasks are accomplished by which positions and in what sequence.
- Hand-offs between functions, departments or individuals.
- Internal and outsourced operational limits or boundaries.
- Start and stop points.

Other charting tools include workflow or functional diagrams.

A process map is developed to first better understand gaps, such as cost, speed, quality, or service, in any key area of the business. The second reason process maps are so effective is that once you have drawn a picture of what a process looks like, most people understand it much better and faster. The result is closing the gaps by creating a more effective process.

A typical process map:

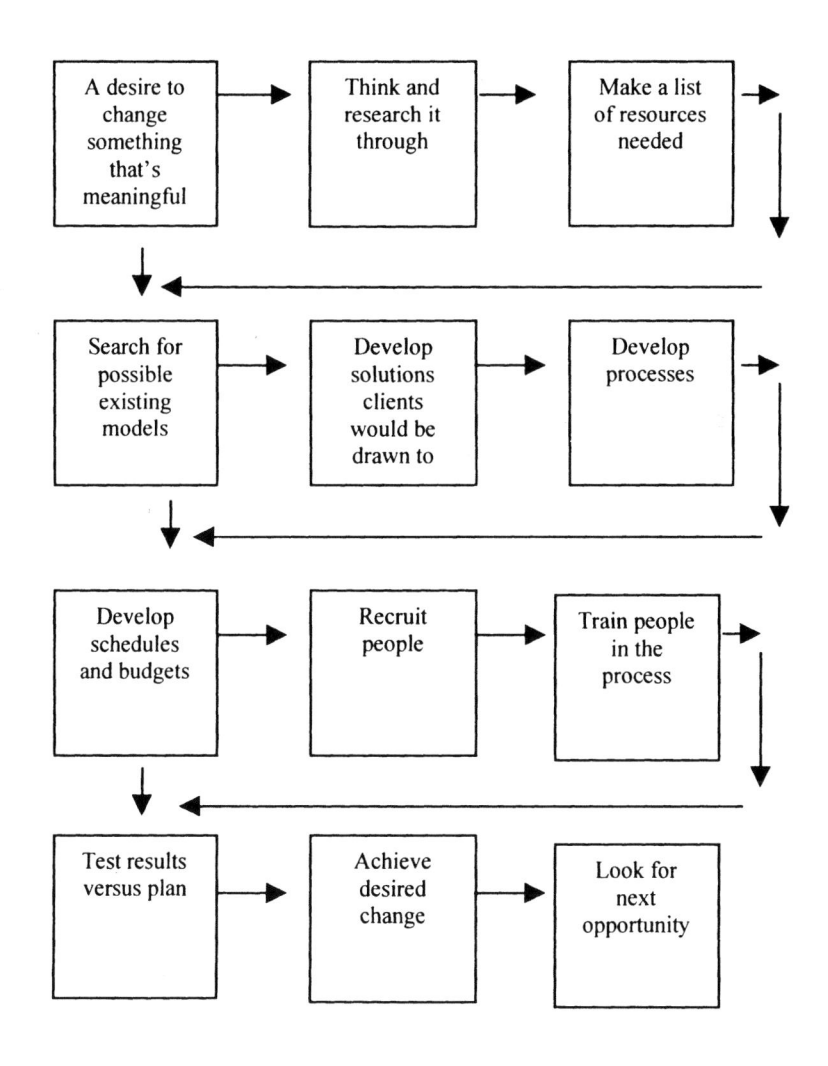

```
┌──────────────┐    ┌──────────────┐    ┌──────────────┐
│ A desire to  │ →  │ Think and    │ →  │ Make a list  │ →
│ change       │    │ research it  │    │ of resources │
│ something    │    │ through      │    │ needed       │  │
│ that's       │    │              │    │              │  ↓
│ meaningful   │    │              │    │              │
└──────────────┘    └──────────────┘    └──────────────┘
      │    ←─────────────────────────────────────────────
      ↓
┌──────────────┐    ┌──────────────┐    ┌──────────────┐
│ Search for   │ →  │ Develop      │ →  │ Develop      │ →
│ possible     │    │ solutions    │    │ processes    │
│ existing     │    │ clients      │    │              │  │
│ models       │    │ would be     │    │              │  ↓
│              │    │ drawn to     │    │              │
└──────────────┘    └──────────────┘    └──────────────┘
      │    ←─────────────────────────────────────────────
      ↓
┌──────────────┐    ┌──────────────┐    ┌──────────────┐
│ Develop      │ →  │ Recruit      │ →  │ Train people │ →
│ schedules    │    │ people       │    │ in the       │
│ and budgets  │    │              │    │ process      │  │
│              │    │              │    │              │  ↓
└──────────────┘    └──────────────┘    └──────────────┘
      │    ←─────────────────────────────────────────────
      ↓
┌──────────────┐    ┌──────────────┐    ┌──────────────┐
│ Test results │ →  │ Achieve      │ →  │ Look for     │
│ versus plan  │    │ desired      │    │ next         │
│              │    │ change       │    │ opportunity  │
└──────────────┘    └──────────────┘    └──────────────┘
```

The Process for Creating a Process Map

1. Select a gap that's important.

2. Select team members closest to performing the task.

3. Visually observe each step and diagram it out by drawing a box around each task.

4. Add position responsible timing or other standards in each box, moving from left to right

Once you have agreement from all the team members, analyze the total process map for non-value added. See if there are any steps that need to be eliminated or possibly duplicated, or if you need to change the standard order.

Next, document all changes into a new process map and validate improvements by measuring the results. Again, you're looking for unnecessary steps, rework, consolidation, or new and better technology. When doing these steps, make sure you do not threaten the people. Remember what Peter Drucker said many years ago, "It's not the people; it's the process."

When doing your first process map, start with something that's easy. Sell and educate your workers on the new process, and always lead, don't dictate. Realize that change must be sold to one person at a time. People don't resist change as much as they resist being changed.

Finally, we all know that small, privately owned businesses have a lot to offer. Many companies have great products and services, but most small businesses don't take the time to develop all the critical processes necessary to achieve the unlimited earnings potential they could achieve. This isn't because owners and managers don't want to grow, but because most of them never received the necessary interactive management and marketing processes' team training necessary to know what to do and exactly how to do it.

But all that's about to change. As I share these concepts about the synergy factor with you, you'll soon have the tools necessary to create the business of your dreams. Let's begin.

Chapter One

The First Step to High Performance

"Everything depends on what the people are capable of wanting."
                                            - Enrico Malatesta
"Man is what he believes."

                                            - Anton Chekho

While running a small business can be both difficult and unpredictable, it's also one of the most exciting things you can do. Having total control of your life, developing a residual income, and fulfilling a need in the community or marketplace are all powerful motivators to business ownership.

If you are proud of your business accomplishments so far, you deserve full credit. Since so few businesses survive the long-term, you should be pleased that your efforts are achieving your desired results. However, if your business, to this point, has not been as successful as you'd like it to be, then you only have yourself to blame, not the business, not your people, not your customers, not the economy, and not your financial situation. Ultimately, you and your key managers are responsible for every business decision and resulting consequence, whether good or bad.

Although that may sound harsh, especially if you're working as hard as you can, it's actually great news. It proves that you have the power to move beyond your current level of success (or lack of it) and build your business exactly the way you want it to be. From this point on, there are no excuses, because failing with an excuse (even a really good one) is still failing. If you're finished with excuses and have decided to reach for your highest potential, then the information in this book will help you reach the success level you desire . . . and deserve!

The fact is that every business in the world can reach new heights of success, whether it's a start-up, a 20-year old well-established corporation producing sales of $50,000,000, or anything in-between. No matter where your business currently is, if you're a serious business owner or key manager, this book will reveal the steps to achieving the next level of success. Depending on your industry and current revenue, achieving the next level could mean any of the following:

- Increasing profits.

- Having more time off.

- Being debt-free.

- Having others run the business for you.

- Creating a world-class, international company.

- Having total security and freedom.

- Increasing your income and net worth.

- Preparing the business to sell.

- Building residual income.

To pinpoint your specific goals, ask yourself the following questions:

- Have you ever been frustrated because your sales aren't growing like you know they could be?

- Have you ever been disappointed because your people didn't get the job done on time, and you lost a customer because of it?

- Have you ever wondered why your profit margins aren't growing like you want them (and need them) to?

- Have you ever wondered why your employees don't do what you ask?

- Have you ever wondered where the cash is at year-end, after taxes?

If you answered "yes" to any of the above questions, you're ready to learn about the synergy factor and how it can be your key to business success. When you choose to develop and implement the synergy factor into your business, you eliminate all the above frustrations and enter a whole new environment of business. As a result, you begin to realize that your job as a business owner or key manager is not to do the work or constantly solve problems; rather, your job is to build a company that does the work *for* you. You begin to think about how the team can use the process to solve the problems and increase the profits.

When you create the processes and train each functional team on their implementation and day-to-day operation, you'll be able to accomplish the following:

- Motivate people so they stay with you and increase their productivity.

- Eliminate common problems by empowering people to identify and solve them once and for all.

- Get jobs done on time, every time, exactly as you promised.

- Decrease costs as redos and errors disappear.

- Create a key management team that is trained and qualified to run the business for you.

- Increase sales through the development of powerful and effective marketing, advertising, public relations, and sales processes.

- Increase customer loyalty.

- Weed out time wasting activities.

- Build a better life for yourself and your people.

Additionally, when you have more time and money to achieve your personal goals, you'll eventually be able to do one of the following: sell the business for a great profit, keep the business and run it problem-free, or create lifetime income by running the business as an investor rather than as an employee. Ultimately, the more successful your business becomes, the more time you have for your personal endeavors and less stress you have on the job.

Process Driven Teams are The Key

Process teams are the single most important requirement for creating great relationships and achieving better results while exerting less effort and utilizing less time. Unfortunately, most business training employs a piecemeal approach. There's no team or process training. However, you have probably noticed that when you take the time to develop a written method of getting something done, train the people to follow it, and then measure the results on a frequent basis, the job gets done right, on budget, and on time, even though you didn't do it yourself.

The fact is that most consulting companies and seminars address the symptoms of business failure; they don't solve the problems. When work is not done correctly, when goals are not achieved, or when good people quit, your employees are not to blame. Since there are no process teams established—no written documents for them to follow—they simply cannot be successful in their job.

Choose to be A Synergy Factor Team Leader

Most owners and key managers of small to mid-size businesses can only dream of the day when they have complete freedom and can focus on the tasks they love to do. Rather than spending hundreds of hours solving the same problems or worrying about sales and profits, they long for the day when they can concentrate on taking their business to the next level of success. If you want the success you dream about, then you have to develop the processes and teams necessary to eliminate your common day-to-day problems and increase profits.

No matter what industry you're in, it's only logical to identify and prioritize your problems so you can create the processes necessary for getting the job done right the first time. Spending your time and energy convincing people to do the job right and then watching them fail is counterproductive, to say the least.

Maybe it seems unreasonable to expect people to meet your standards, but I've never heard of a business that failed because of setting standards too high. In fact, becoming a process-based manager means raising everyone's standards. It means expecting higher levels of performance in every key area of the business, from sales and marketing to operations, from finance to management and leadership.

Process-based teams involve an exchange between employees and customers about problems and possible solutions that add value to the relationship. If you don't quantify the problems in terms of what it's costing not to solve them, you can't prioritize which problems to solve first. In effect, the quantification question is the single most powerful way to get people's attention. This exchange provides a reliable way for discovering, within five minutes, whether an employee or a customer is worth pursuing.

So if you're ready to make a difference in your business and become a better business owner or manager in the process, this book is for you. You'll learn new concepts and valuable ideas to make your business a success. Now is the perfect time to make The Synergy Factor work for you.

Chapter Two

Why 96% of all Businesses Eventually Fail

"Nothing is more terrible than activity without insight."
- Thomas Carlyle

The statistics are startling, only four percent of all businesses survive long term. How is that possible? Consider this: approximately one million businesses are started each year. In the first 10 years, 80% of those businesses close their doors. Within the next twenty years, 90% of the remaining businesses will shut down.

Family-owned businesses don't rate much better. Seventy percent of second generation family businesses fail. And third and fourth generation businesses are very rare. In fact, of the original Dow thirty, only one has survived (General Electric).

This year alone, over 400,000 businesses will go bankrupt while countless others will simply close their doors. Unfortunately, most business owners don't see this tragedy coming until it is too late. By the time many owners realize how serious their problems are, they simply can't do anything to salvage their hopes for success.

Why is it that so many businesses fail? Research conducted over the past 20 years has discovered that over 90% of the businesses that have failed neglected to address ten key problems. Namely:

1. They can't develop sales fast enough.

2. They can't reduce costs effectively.

3. They can't increase profits every year.

4. They can't recruit quality people, resulting in capacity issues.

5. They can't retain quality people, resulting in cost and quality issues.

6. Customer satisfaction decreases, resulting in lost sales.

7. The business is too dependent on a few key people.

8. They can't increase cash flow, resulting in increasing debt load.

9. The business doesn't change with the times (strategy problem).

10. There is no management succession plan, resulting in the inability to grow and sell the business.

What's really unfortunate is that every problem listed has a solution. And the only difference between success and failure lies in the owner's attitude—the ability to change their way of thinking on how to solve these problems.

What is the cost of not solving the problems listed above? Any one of the above problems will cause a business to eventually fail. Two or three of the above problems occurring simultaneously can take any business down in less than three years. And four or more of these problems will close a business in 18 months or less, depending on how deep the owner's pockets are or how much debt occurs before the cash runs out.

The real problem, however, is in the mind of the owner and his or her advisors. If the business owner doesn't open up to a new way of thinking about how to solve these problems, the problems will eventually overcome the business. But it doesn't have to be this way.

In his best selling book *Unlimited Wealth*, Paul Pilzer, the Nobel Prize winning economist, says that technology is the major determination of wealth. And the advance of technology is determined mainly by our ability to process information.

Technology is defined as science, and science is defined as the acquisition of knowledge that can be measured precisely. In other words, **unlimited wealth is determined by your organization's ability to acquire knowledge that can be measured.**

This also holds true for labor. The productive value of a person is in direct proportion to their level of education and knowledge toward doing their job better and faster. The implication of not educating managers and teams is the cause of 90% of all business problems. In every small business, the number one priority for top management is to make sure they increase middle and lower management's knowledge so it can be measured for the purpose of doing the job better and faster. This process has proven to be the best way to create increased wealth for everyone involved, from employee to owner.

The More You Know, The More Fun You Can Have
After you own or manage a company for any amount of time, you find out it isn't always what you expected it would be. You either hate the job or you love the job. There isn't much in between.

After thirty years in business, I have worked in companies of all sizes—from huge businesses with sales of over fifty billion dollars to medium-sized businesses with sales of one hundred million dollars to small businesses with sales from one to fifty million dollars. I have worked in companies where there was nothing but problems and even the simplest task posed quite a challenge. However, I have also worked in companies where the day-to-day activities were challenging, exciting, and downright fun.

Your organization's culture plays a large role in how you feel about your company. The organizational culture you want involves recruiting and selecting the right people. I define the right people as having a mindset of being open minded and asking questions in order to get it right. You want team players who enjoy doing that kind of work.

On average, I consult as many as twenty businesses at a time, working with their managers to improve their performance. I'll admit, it's hard work. But would it really be fun if it were easy? I doubt it. My purpose in business is to find those owners and managers who are challenged by the game of business and who want to spend the next few years trying to master it.

Whether you're an owner or a manager, you have no doubt learned the ropes. You can probably deal effectively with producing the products and services. You may even feel comfortable with most of what you are doing. So what's left to learn?

After working with over 200 companies, I have identified five areas of team knowledge that are relevant to business success. They are:

1. The Leadership and Management Teams

Leadership and management are two different skill sets. Your leadership ability is directly related to your dream of the future and is accomplished through the establishment and development of powerful goals for yourself and your company. Management, on the other hand, is directly related to your organizational delegation and process development. If you develop an organizational strategy, job descriptions, work standards, measured accountability, and a coaching method that focuses these skills on the achievement of your leadership goals, you will successfully increase your ability to achieve those goals.

Leadership ability is also related to your unique ability. If you focus on your unique ability you can operate successfully in any situation, regardless of the economy, competition, people problems, or changes in your life. You can then instill your beliefs in others and lead them to attaining their goals as well. By developing the leadership and management skills of your key management team you will begin to grow to greater and greater levels of achievement. And if you want to be really good, then you develop these skills in yourself, because if you want to create extraordinary success you must develop yourself before developing others.

2. The Operations Team

Operations success is directly related to your ability to get your products and services completed on time, at the lowest creation cost, exactly as promised or your customers' money back. If you focus on the development of documented proven processes for the design, production, quality control, elimination of redos and errors, and delivery, you will create customer loyalty, develop a highly motivated workforce, and increase profits regardless of what the competition does.

3. The Financial and Information Team

Your financial ability is directly related to developing an accurate chart of accounts, a contribution method financial statement, a realistic budget, a ratio analysis versus your industry standards, a cash plan, a job profit plan, a people profit plan, a company net worth growth plan and process value assessments reports.

4. The Marketing and Sales Team

Sales and marketing are two different skill sets that are commonly confused. Sales involves getting your product into your customer's hands. It's the ability to exchange your product for money. However, your marketing ability is directly related to your product versus market segment match potential and your competitive advantage potential. It also involves understanding how your customers think and make decisions. It's the written marketing strategy that includes the messages, the products, the promotions, the channels, and the budget. Most important, your

...keting should be based on customer research and what customers want versus what you may think they want. It's the constant measurement of these strategies versus goals and the innovation of each variable that creates a sales and marketing process that achieves results.

5. The Advertising and Public Relations Teams

Advertising is the ability to convert the marketing strategy into a message and channel strategy that creates enough qualified prospects to maximize the sales department's time and effectiveness. Smart advertising enables you to achieve new sales goals at the lowest cost.

Public relations is your ability to relate to your customers. When you can do this, you're able to convert leads into appointments for needs analysis/opportunity meetings and solution presentations (based on accurate estimates of price, quality, and time the customer agrees with). The ultimate goal is to convert that lead into a sale. It's the constant measurement of these processes versus goals and the innovation of each variable that creates a sales force that achieves results.

These five areas include problem solving, training, recruiting, selecting, mentoring, innovation, and measuring processes. As you and your teams complete each of the five critical areas of process development, your confidence in your company's ability to achieve its goals regardless of what happens to the economy, people, competition, or you will increase. Once you have a firm grasp on these areas, your business's performance will skyrocket and you'll have more fun along the way.

Plan for Smarter Choices

When I was in my twenties, I got interested in management. At the time, I was fresh out of the Army and working as a sales clerk in the men's department at a large Detroit department store, the J.L. Hudson Company.

I started at the bottom, at minimum wage. I didn't have much going for me at the time—no college degree and no retail industry knowledge. I found myself in a situation that needed improvement. I learned every part of my job by reading the operating manuals and practicing each job until I was excellent at it.

I soon realized that the higher paid people were either in management positions or had a skilled trade, such as big-ticket sales. I decided to shoot for acquiring management skills, so I got an appointment with the top manager of our department and told him I had an idea to help our sales slump.

I revealed to him that we didn't really attract the teen market to our department, but rather the mothers of those teens. I knew our sales could increase if we could somehow attract that younger crowd to our store. So I showed him a list of clothes our competitors were carrying, and added that the presence of a jukebox and rock and roll graphics in the old, plain department would attract the teen market. I was surprised when he gave me the authority to purchase the new clothing lines while he took care of the graphics and jukebox.

In less than six months of introducing the new line, the department's sales took off. I was promoted to assistant department manager and entered into Hudson's management training. This opportunity helped me to gain management skills and led to other jobs with more responsibility.

But that wasn't the only time my planning paid off. In 1989, four years after starting our company, we had reached a growth slump. Sales and profits were at a stalemate.

I observed that our clients knew how to do the operating end of their business but not many knew the management end of business. I began drawing on the years of experience I had obtained while working for large corporations. By combining all that knowledge and experience, I was able to devise a new service—management training—to offer my clients. I developed the processes to make it happen. I devoted 10 hours a week to develop training processes and details of the new service I offered.

In the next 12 months I broke through every sales and profit record and made more profits than I had my first two years in business. Planning and processes worked again! And best of all, I had fun the entire time.

At this point in my life, I wouldn't trade anything for my 15 years working in large companies, because it has served as the foundation for my present career. The experience was invaluable.

Had I not had the opportunity to get effective training in management and marketing processes, my life would probably be very different today. And this is the problem many people have. They think they would like a certain job, or to be a business owner, but they don't really know what the person in that position does. Therefore, they often find that they made a bad choice or they are not achieving the results they want. They are constantly faced with a pattern of problems, such as "I can't increase sales at the rate we need to," "I can't find enough good people to get the work done on time," "There are too many redos and errors," or "I can't achieve the profit or cash flow necessary to grow a business I can be proud of."

Do you ever ask yourself any of the following questions:

- Am I really inspiring my people?

- Am I really prioritizing my work correctly?

- Am I really doing what a person in this position is supposed to be doing to be as effective as I could be?

- Do I have all the knowledge necessary to increase sales, profits, and cash flow?

- Do I have the bonus incentive that will motivate people to increase profits and achieve goals?

If these questions plague you, then you're not achieving all you can in your business. So to be a really great entrepreneur or manager, you need to know exactly what people in your position do and how they do it. That way you can have every advantage to be as successful as you want to be and have fun doing it!

What Owners and Managers Do: Illusion versus Reality

If you read most "how to" books, go back to college, or attend most seminars, they will all tell you the same thing. Managers don't work—they get work done by other people. It doesn't take a rocket scientist to understand how simplistic and unhelpful this definition is. Dictators, tyrants, bullies, and politicians get work done by other people. What actually happens in many businesses is quite different than what is taught in most books, schools, or seminars.

Illusion #1 – The manager is a strategic thinker.
The reality is that the manager is actually working very hard on activities characterized by brevity, variety, and mostly without written processes. They are in the habit of doing something versus taking the time to create a measurable process that will work best over time.

Illusion #2 – The manager obtains accurate information and keeps communications clear to everyone.
The reality is that managers strongly favor meetings and telephone calls. They are rarely facilitators of one-to-one information exchanges and would rather disperse information through "the pipeline."

Illusion #3 – Management is a profession.
In reality, management itself is a part of any job—it's not a job unto itself. In fact, how managers do their work, schedule their time, process information, make decisions, and so on, is all in their heads. There is no profession of purely "management."

Position Functions

The work a manager or team does can best be described as the results expected according to the organization of the company in its organizational chart (most businesses don't have a current or accurate organizational chart they follow). An example of those positions might be operations manager, sales manager, finance manager, president, and so on. By virtue of position as head of a functional department, every manager performs what he or she believes is the best way to get work done and achieve every goal.

Managers are supposed to be in control in the sense of getting results from people. And since control is defined as comparing where you are to where you're supposed to be, you can take corrective action when there is a gap. So naturally, it follows that if you have no process, you cannot have control, since you have no documented, measured step-by-step method with standards to follow. For that reason, process mapping and measurement is not an option–it is a requirement. When management spends more time mapping critical processes, there are fewer businesses operating in crisis mode and failing in such huge numbers, even after twenty or more years in business.

Make the Time for Success

Most business problems occur because of a lack of effective processes, a lack of trained and dedicated people, the inability to measure the results of all the critical processes, and neglecting to act on the variable. Owners and key managers fail to focus enough time with their people in the process of continuous improvement and the tracking of critical processes and correct strategy.

The answers to solving business problems begin when top management understands that the people who do the work must be empowered to have meaningful input into how that work is to be done. Additionally, top management must be sure their strategy is right. The only ways to make this happen are 1) to reduce the amount of time owners and managers spend doing the job and increase the amount of time spent educating their people on process mapping and accountability, and 2) to research and quantify their concept in the market place.

The idea is to spend time process mapping versus putting out fires—to create a business that will run by process. Unfortunately, most small business owners believe they are too busy to take the time to develop these key process maps. They spend so much time focusing on the day-to-day activities that they can no longer see the big picture—their goal to create a business that can run itself and provide a steady stream of income. If you don't take the time to create your processes—your success strategy—your business will not survive the long-term.

Owners must realize that a business isn't just a group of people doing work. It should be a business process that is operated by people. The process does the work and the people follow the process. Without processes in place, a small business depends on one or two people to keep it running. If they leave or get sick for even a short amount of time, the business is thrown off. Additionally, those few people cannot grow the business until they can replace themselves. But if you have the right processes in place, the teams can run the business. And that is the real secret behind every small business that grew big.

Now that you understand the importance of developing key processes to make your business run smoother, we'll look at the various functions in detail. This will help you understand how each component plays an important role to your business's overall success.

Part II

Chapter Three

The First Synergy Factor

"If the blind lead the blind, both shall fall into the ditch."
— The Bible (Matthew 15:14)

The Leadership & Management Team: The Keys to Happy and Productive Employees

Retaining and motivating your key employees while increasing their productivity is what leadership and management processes are all about. It's one key aspect to the whole synergy factor. Why is this so important? Quite simply, without the right people and the know-how to select, lead and manage them, your business can't survive the long-term.

Unfortunately, the recent economic climate makes attracting and keeping good employees difficult. In fact, research shows that a critical shortage of quality people is the number one concern among most business owners and key managers today. And this shortage of quality people is forecasted to continue for many more years.

Additionally, the average cost of turnover is calculated at somewhere between $10,000 - $15,000 per person. How is this possible? Consider this: according to the U.S. Department of Labor, it costs a company one-third of a new hire's annual salary to replace an employee. So using a modest annual salary of $35,000, a company can easily spend $11,550 for each new employee hired.

This figure comprises both direct and indirect costs. Direct costs include advertising expenses and headhunter fees, as well as management's time involved in recruitment, selection, and training. Indirect costs include overtime expenses and possibly decreased productivity while current employees pick up the slack until the new hire is up to speed.

Even worse, some key positions are almost impossible to replace, such as the vice president who has been with the company for 20 or more years and is the true brains behind the operation, or even the secretary who assists an entire department and keeps key people on track with ease. When quality people like this leave, capacity is reduced, profits can decline, and customers are often lost.

When asked why they believe people leave their organization, most owners or managers cite money as the most important motivator. However, quite the opposite is true. In fact, the three biggest reasons why good employees leave are 1) they believe the company lacks long term growth potential, 2) they are not growing as individuals, or 3) they feel as if no one cares about them.

Each of these three problems stems from a lack of leadership and management processes. When the management team is not giving employees the feedback, training, guidance, motivation, and recognition they deserve, many employees will seek employment elsewhere, despite their current salary, position title, company car, corner office, or any other material incentive the business can afford.

For example, employees may believe the company lacks growth potential because there is no written and communicated strategic long term plan, profit plan, how are we doing report, or other regularly updated communications events to keep them informed.

Likewise, employees believe they have no personal growth potential in a company because the company has not developed a future organizational chart, position agreements, or personal development education and training opportunities to give them something to strive for.

Additionally, employees believe no one cares about them because the company has no formal mentoring process and no leadership or management processes that teach managers how to deal with and communicate effectively with people. No one spends quality time with the people who do the work.

Obviously, retaining and motivating people while increasing productivity is a critical challenge today. Without quality people you can't stay in business, and without increasing productivity you can't increase profits.

Productivity Strategy

Paul Pilzer, the Nobel Prize winning economist, makes the following statement in his great classic book *Unlimited Wealth*: "All wealth in the next ten years will be created by technology with its ability to get the work done faster at ever increasing levels of quality. This can only be accomplished by allocating more time and investment towards the education of the workforce."

When companies don't increase their productivity, they've failed to motivate and train their employees how to develop high goals and how to quantify and achieve those goals. When you create effective processes that eliminate redos and errors while rewarding people when they achieve goals, you will increase productivity every time. The effective development of leadership and management processes takes time, but the return on training as an investment is indeed measurable. Research from some of the best companies in America shows returns of 30%, 50%, 100% and more.

The seven leadership and management processes that produce the highest productivity are as follows:

1. Hire The Right People In The First Place

The best way to ensure that you have qualified and motivated employees is to selectively hire people based on a set of written and enforced standards. When you identify key personality and work ethic traits that a person in a particular position must possess, you can match your candidates with those requirements and can always be confident that you're hiring the best person for the job. Since most people are creatures of habit, how they act when you first meet them is often how they will act for the duration of their employment with you. Try as you may, you won't be able to transform a mediocre hire into a stellar employee. The key is to have a hiring process and hire smart from the beginning.

2. Train Cross Functional Teams

Those employees who actually do the work must be empowered to make decisions that affect their workload and job performance. Obviously, employees can't make every decision on their own. After all, that's what managers are trained to do. However, if you want to retain your employees, develop a process that outlines the kinds of decisions employees and work teams can make for themselves and the kinds of decisions that must be left to management. The more your employees feel empowered, the more motivated they will become.

3. Pay Bonuses Contingent on Increased Profits

While money isn't your employees' greatest motivator, it does have some bearing on their overall outlook and job satisfaction. To make sure your employees are being fairly compensated, regularly research what the average salary is for each position in your company. Next, outline the specific objectives each person must attain in order to receive a pay increase and communicate those objectives to your employees. When employees don't understand how job performance relates to salary, they begin to believe that unfair compensation practices exist. As a result, they view their lower salary as a personal affront rather than a job performance issue, and they'll want to leave your company. Develop bonus incentives for individual achievement and total organizational performance.

4. Develop More Opportunity and Job Security

Your employees want to know that they'll have a job today, tomorrow, next week, and even next year. However, if you don't document where the employee's current position could lead and offer training for the employee to attain that status, he or she will eventually feel as if the current position is not valued and has no growth potential. Additionally, should a particular department close for whatever reason, your employees want to be reassured that they'll be able to transfer to another position. That's why having a process of cross-training each employee is so crucial.

5. Training in Technical and Human Development

In order to keep your employees as valued members of your team; training is a vital component. The more training your employees have, the more confident they'll be in their job duties, often resulting in higher quality output on their part. In order to be effective, training needs to be given consistently. To do this, detail who will give the training, who needs to receive it, and precisely what the training will consist of. This will ensure that each person receives the same information, so there's never any question as to who learned what in the training session.

6. Create a Team Environment

Employees want to feel as if they're part of a team, not a subservient member of an organization. They also want to know that they can progress to higher levels through experience, training, and performance, even if they don't possess the educational background typically required for the position. In order to foster this team environment, business owners in many industries have status distinctions. Rather, through the use of documented organizational charts, they let employees know how each person stands in the company by function. This type of environment allows for an open exchange of ideas regardless of position or ranking. The result is more creativity from your employees and more open communication between management and workers.

7. Communication and Open Book Management

To motivate your employees, it's important to keep them updated on what is happening financially and functionally. If employees feel they're being excluded from information that directly affects them, they'll quickly become unmotivated. For example, imagine how irate employees would be learning from another employee that their company hit their goals rather than hearing the news from their direct supervisor or company reports. To keep communication lines open, create a process for dispersing information in a timely manner. Whether you choose to communicate via formal or informal meetings, email, bulletin board postings, etc. is up to you and contingent upon what will work best in your unique organization. The purpose is to keep the communication consistent and accurate so employees are continually updated on the company's critical numbers and news.

Unfortunately, many businesses employ the above leadership and management processes in a piecemeal approach. The problem with this is that any one or two of the above by themselves don't have nearly the effect as doing them all at the same time. For example, what good is it to train employees if they don't know how they fit in the big picture or how they can use their new skills to advance from their current position? Similarly, why should employees even want to bother with additional training if they feel as if they don't have job opportunity or any say in decisions that affect their job? And why would a prospective job candidate who you are selectively hiring want to work for you if you're known for keeping your employees uninformed of company status?

Obviously, it takes time to implement these processes and see real results. It takes time to train and upgrade the skills of your existing workforce and even more time to see the economic benefit. However, taking this "long view" is absolutely essential to creating a high performance organization.

The Difference Between Leadership and Management

With all this discussion of leadership and management processes, many people may be wondering what's the difference between managers and leaders. Quite simply, tasks need to be managed; people need to be led. Any component that involves a task requires a management process, while any component that involves people requires a leadership process.

Unfortunately, many owners and managers try to manage people rather than lead them to the desired outcome. A true leader is a motivator. The best leaders know that they communicate a vision for a great future. Their passion and attitude sets the energy for everyone in the company. They focus on building people and developing teams that will move the company ahead. They know that their number one priority is to be sure that everyone is in the process of continually improving results. They take the time to go through the ongoing process of documenting policy and procedure, measuring the success of those procedures, and taking the necessary steps to make sure everyone in the organization is mentored and trained on a regular basis.

Leaders set objectives in advance. They put objectives in writing. They focus on measuring sales growth, profits, productivity, and cash flow. They are dynamic; revising the objectives in response to major changes and trends.

Managers who lead rather than manage create an environment where people feel important—a place where they can learn, grow, and feel motivated to contribute. They place honesty, fairness, persistence, predictability, patience, compassion, and a commitment of improvement above all else.

Managing, on the other hand, focuses on the tasks to be done rather than the people who do it. Managers evaluate the current processes and process the needed requirements in order to ensure the desired outcomes. Managing focuses on the end result rather than the vision to get there. This is not to say that management is not as important as leadership or that leadership is better than management. They're simply two different processes, and your business needs both to survive.

The Leadership and Management Synergy Factor Will Keep Your Doors Open

After many years in business, most business owners and managers are concerned about two things: 1) the ability to grow profits in the future at the levels necessary to pay themselves and their employees the income that will provide the lifestyle they desire, and 2) the ability to build stock value so the owners can get a return on their investment when they sell the business. The answer to both these concerns is to train key management teams in leadership, management, and information processes that are constantly measured and innovated.

A poll we completed showed that over 90% of managers have received little or no training in leadership, management, finance or team building. Yet these same people are expected to lead, manage, and increase profits. Every occupation in the world knows that educating and training people is critical to success in any profession, be it engineering, carpentry, tool making, or project management. Every large corporation spends millions of dollars on management training, but the average small business owner fails to understand that he/she must do the same at a level they can afford. Businesses fail to grow continually, generation after generation, because they fail to understand this fact of life.

If no one teaches people the leadership, management, and financial processes required to grow to the next level, the company will stop growing at some point. If these problems are not corrected, the business will face the ultimate disaster: bankruptcy or closing.

The good news is that anyone who wants to grow can learn how. Leadership skills include how to set goals for yourself and others in order to inspire people to perform at higher levels. Leadership skills also include time management, innovation, team building, and character development. Management skills include how to develop an organizational team strategy that can achieve every objective. Other skills include mentoring, recruiting, organizing, writing position descriptions with standards, facilitating effective meetings, and writing the processes necessary to train people to do a better job.

Financial skills include understanding all the numbers, from the income statement to the balance sheet. When employees are trained in financial skills, they understand precisely how they can help the company reduce costs and increase profits. Additionally, when managers have a firm grasp of financial skills, they can design an incentive process that rewards people where it counts most: in higher profits.

Too many business owners assume that the employees already possess these skills, but the truth is that most employees don't know them. To make matters worse, they don't want their boss to think they don't know, so they blame others or the economy for their failures so they don't lose their job. They don't ask for more training because they don't want to appear incompetent. Sometimes they may not even be aware that they lack these skills, but the result is the same–failure to grow sales or profits or cash flow or people.

If the needed leadership and management processes were in place, the employees would never feel incompetent because training would be unified and consistent. Additionally, employees would know their value to the company and how their job function affects the big picture and impacts sales, even if they don't have any direct customer contact.

Furthermore, when training procedures are documented, key managers would know how to train and motivate their employees in order to increase productivity and ultimately the bottom line. The result would be a more streamlined and stress-free environment where everyone knows what's needed to get the job done correctly and on time.

Develop Scorecards

To achieve and sustain success you must measure more than just the short-term finance goals this particular process helps you attain. By developing scorecards and tracking your progress, you can measure customer satisfaction and the value of processes, meet shareholder needs, discover ways to improve productivity, communicate progress, and create a link to performance bonus and incentive programs.

Scorecards can include goals versus actual, or improvement versus history. The data should focus on critical numbers at a frequency level that makes everyone totally knowledgeable on a timely basis. The idea is to track the progress of a particular process so you can streamline it even further and best utilize it to contribute to your synergy factor.

The Leadership and Management Synergy Factor Works

There is definite evidence that investments in leadership and management process maps and employee training can locate flaws in your current job profiles, evaluate activities, mobilize teams to streamline and improve processes, and identify processes that need to be reengineered. A major study conducted during 1996, 1997, and 1998 found that companies that developed leadership and management processes and that invested on average $1,595 per employee in training experienced 24% higher gross profit margins, 218% higher income per employee, and 26% higher stock price to book ratios.

With the current labor shortage, it's interesting to also note that recruitment and retention of employees was much improved. Companies that invested in processes and training dramatically reduced turnover and increased employee satisfaction.

But be advised that your processes can't begin and end with leadership and management training. In fact, leadership and management processes are just one small piece of the pie. In order to grow your business, increase profits, and attract new customers, you need to implement processes in every part of your business, as each process impacts another. If you simply pick and choose which processes you want to implement, inefficiency and waste will still prevail, rob your organization of profits, and result in most of the problems you experience over and over again.

In the next chapter we'll build on the leadership and management synergy factor by discussing sales and marketing processes. You'll discover how one affects the other and learn how combining the processes can help your business grow.

Chapter Four

The Second Synergy Factor

"Research is to see what everybody else has seen, and to think what nobody else has thought."
                    - Albert Szent-Gyorgyi

"It used to be that people needed products to survive. Now products need people to survive."
                    - Nicholas Johnson

The Sales and Marketing Team – The Lifeblood of Your Business

If the world defines the entrepreneur as America's new hero, it's easy to understand why. All the real job growth and wealth created in the last ten years and projected for the next ten to come is fueled by the extraordinary growth of small companies into mid-sized companies.

The growth process usually begins when the business moves from 3-10 employees or sales of $600,000 to $2,500,000 to a mid-sized business with 15-25 employees or sales of $2,600,000 to $10,000,000, and then to a corporate business with 25-100 employees or sales of $11,000,000 to $50,000,000 annually.

Most entrepreneurs in business today realize that growth transitions must take place to ensure long-term profits.

In order to attain the growth they desire, these professionals realize that sales and marketing are the lifeblood of their business. After all, if they can't sell or market their products and services to the intended customers, there's little chance for success. That's why so many highly successful business owners focus on sales and marketing right from the start.

Unfortunately, most owners and managers don't differentiate between the sales and marketing functions of their business. They combine the two functions together and assume that their people can do sales just as efficiently as marketing. However, as mentioned earlier, sales and marketing are two entirely different skill sets.

Marketing versus Sales

Marketing involves promoting your products and services to your intended audience. It's about gaining name recognition, building product or service interest, and understanding how your customers think. When you're marketing your business, no selling is taking place; you're simply paving the way for future sales.

The sales occur after marketing. Sales involves exchanging your products or services for money. The selling process includes speaking one-to-one with your customers, finding their needs, and addressing their concerns. Sales is a two-way dialog with customers while marketing is a one-way exchange.

The problems occur when owners and managers confuse and/or combine the two processes. They start selling before any marketing has been done. When this happens, customers have no prior exposure to the products—no name recognition—causing the selling process to be unbearably long. Considering that sales research conducted by Harvard University indicates that new prospects need to hear about your product or service six to seven times before making a buying decision, selling before marketing is counterproductive, to say the least.

Branding is a Vital Component

Branding is your company's ability to make a promise of distinction. It is what separates your company from your competitors and makes you stand out as different and more valuable to the target market segment. The value of your brand is that it instills confidence in your customer's purchase decision.

The foundation to building your brand is in the development of at least three unique selling points. The consistent use of color, graphics, or even a spokesperson can be used to communicate the brand, but they are not the brand itself. Some examples include The Kentucky Colonel or Orville Redenbacker. Others include "Delivery in 30 minutes or less," "Macintosh, the computer for the rest of us," Fed Ex's "Absolutely positively by 10:00 a.m.," "Only from the mind of Minolta," or G.M.'s ""pay me now or pay me more later."

In my 30 years of consulting and training over 200 different businesses in every industry, I have never seen an effective, documented and integrated marketing, advertising, and sales plan. What I have seen are owners who have great product knowledge and some relationship skills, which enables them to grow sales to a point. The problem then is how to transfer those skills to others so they can continue to grow sales when the current sales people can't be there or have transferred to other positions. That's when companies fail. They're unable to grow new sales because the sales and marketing people who started building the relationships with potential customers were unable to pass their successful marketing and selling skills to the next group.

The fact is, if you can't grow sales, then you can't grow profits and you can't grow the business. If you can't grow, then you eventually go out of business. It's just a matter of time.

The Sales Synergy
Sales growth has two areas, new business and existing business.

1. New Business

   There are many reasons why sales don't grow, but the inability to increase leads and then to convert a higher percentage of those leads into paying customers are the two most common reasons for not growing new business. Sales leads don't grow because the market segment, message, or channel is wrong or has changed. All problems related to market segments, messages, or channels are caused by ineffective marketing and advertising strategies. Not being able to convert sales leads into customers is caused by an ineffective sales conversion strategy.

2. Existing Business

The inability to keep good customers and to increase either the size or frequency of each transaction are the two most common reasons for not growing existing sales. Not being able to keep good customers is caused by poor customer satisfaction, which occurs because of either a failure in the sales agreement or in operations. The inability to grow the size and frequency of sales is caused because of poor market segmentation (no client growth), low usage rates, poor product selection, pricing, or inferior customer service.

Most sales organizations fail over time because they lack effective sales and marketing people and processes. In fact, sales and marketing are major problems in the present or near future for most businesses. As discussed earlier, every year approximately 400,000 businesses close their doors and disappear. Many times the services and products these companies offered were good, even excellent. Yet in over half the cases of business failure, low sales was given as the number one reason for failure.

Why does this failure happen? Is it because the salespeople are no good? Is it because the customers won't buy? Is it because there is too much competition?

The answer is no—it's none of those reasons. Sales departments fail because no one has taken the time to research and develop successful marketing and selling processes that can be repeated over and over again. Most marketing and sales people are working on trying to make a sale instead of taking time to develop a process that creates large numbers of quality leads and then converting a large portion of those leads into new profitable sales.

Let me tell you a story. In 1977 a small company recruited me as its new Sales and Marketing Manager. The company had been in business for over twenty years, but sales had stopped growing for the past several. The sales and marketing staff had worked hard to change this. The CEO and other managers had tried to help the sales department, but to no avail. Sales grew less than 3% while the company's expenses continued to grow at a higher rate. Profits were suffering; the trend looked bad. Once I got onboard, what I saw was a lot of experienced people frustrated by the fact that nothing seemed to work any more like the old days.

I began to approach the sales problem the way I had learned while working at larger companies like Alcoa, Chrysler, and J.L. Hudson. In less than nine months after I started my new position as the Sales and Marketing Manager, sales leads began to grow. After eighteen months sales were growing over 20%, and profits increased in similar ratios.

What did I do that no one else had done? It's simple. I went to work on the marketing department instead of the sales department to research, quantify, and plan first a marketing strategy, then an advertising strategy that worked. By taking that approach, the company went on to grow sales over $30,000,000 in the next few years and eventually sold out, creating millions of dollars for the stockholders. Since that time I have repeated this process in numerous companies ranging from job shops, machine shops, construction companies, medical offices, sign shops, law firms, accounting firms, and even service businesses such as contract labor, training, and consulting companies. The success for all these companies lies in selecting, and training the right people and the processes. In all my years of business, I have never seen this approach fail. The first step is to create sales and marketing processes that work, and then train teams to run the processes.

The Selling Synergy That Can Increase Your Income Over 200% in Less than 12 Months

When I started my own company I had no experience selling to business owners and no experience selling the products and services we provided. Since I had purchased a selling process and was trained in how to use it, 50% of my sales success was taken care of. The other 50% came from the records I kept and my daily commitment to following the process. Here are the high points of my sales synergy and how they can work for you.

Part One – The Sales Process

Step 1: Build Prospect Rapport

Most people only do business with those they know, like, and trust. Therefore, before clients do business with you, they need to have a working relationship with you and feel comfortable with you. You build the relationship through phone calls, email, and various other correspondences. The purpose is not to hard sell your business, but rather to let your prospects know that you're available to help when the time is right.

Step 2: Present Your Company's Unique Promise and Product Benefits

During your marketing efforts, be sure to explain what makes your company different from the competition. Is it the customer service you offer, the product quality, your years of experience? Whatever your unique promise is, detail it to your prospects. At the same time, also explain the benefits your products and services can give the prospects. Be sure to differentiate between features and benefits, as the two are completely different. A feature is something your product does or has, while a benefit is how that feature helps the prospect. For example, a feature of a pain medication may be that the tablet is buffered. The benefit is that the tablet won't upset the person's stomach. Since benefits are what appeal to people, stress benefits more than features.

Step 3: Perform a "Gap Analysis" to Uncover Challenges Your Prospects Face Regarding Their Business Situation

In order to know whether or not your product or service will help your prospects, always perform a "gap analysis" of your prospects' problem. You can do this by asking questions, giving surveys, and analyzing any physical data the prospects can supply. The objective is to determine how you and your company can best help the prospects meet their goals.

Step 4: Quantify Each Problem with Some Kind of Value or Number

In order for prospects to buy your solution, they have to know precisely how it will help them. For example, if a prospect's biggest challenge is slow growing sales, you must first identify how far behind the sales are. You can do this with an actual dollar figure or a percentage. Next, determine to what extent your solution can help. So instead of simply stating that your product will help increase sales, state the dollar figure or percentage of increase intended and the specified time period that increase will occur in.

Step 5: Uncover the How, Who, What, When, Where, and Why of Their Customer Base

No matter what you're selling, you can't effectively apply it to your prospects' businesses unless you know the specifics of their clientele. Analyze their current customers' needs and determine how your solution will increase the likelihood of their customers buying more and staying loyal. To learn more about their customers, analyze the customer profiles and sales data on file.

Step 6: Develop a First Draft Solution to the Prospect's Problems

Demonstrate how each of your products and services reduces or eliminates pain through your unique features, benefits, and technical processes (only use those that focus on specific problems the buyer has agreed to). The idea is to be an expert on what your product does. Ask key questions to connect product benefits with buyer needs.

Step 7: Present the First Draft Proposal to Everyone Involved in the Buying Process

Nothing can be more frustrating than delivering a presentation and then learning that key decision-makers were not present. When making your appointment to present your solution, verify that each decision-maker will be there. During the presentation, go through each step of your proposal, asking questions on each item to get agreement and feedback. Compare the cost of the proposal to the potential quantified benefits so your prospects can see the true value of what you're offering.

Step 8: Sharpen Your Proposal

Take note of any feedback you receive during the presentation and incorporate that new data into the proposal's second draft. Make as many draft proposals to the buyer as is necessary before presenting the final proposal.

Step 9: Contact All the Primary Decision-Makers for a Decision

Deliver the final proposal to your primary contact and any other decision-makers. Conduct the presentation in a group setting so it's informal and interactive.

Part Two – Standards in the Sales Process

Below is a list of some standard items you'll want on hand before, during, and after each sales presentation:

- Rapport building cue cards – Set up a file for each prospect. In the file, include note cards that list key information, both personal and professional, about the prospect. Some things you may want to include are spouse's names, professional affiliations, birthdays or anniversaries, and special interests. Whenever you speak with the prospect, use the cue cards to remind yourself to inquire about certain events. This will show your prospects that you care about them more than just as a client.

- Company brochures, videos, etc. – Always keep a supply of business building tools that you can hand out on an as-needed basis. Many times prospects like these items as back-up information sources they can quickly refer to.

- Presentation script – Your script doesn't need to be fully written out or recited verbatim to each prospect. The idea is to have a reference of points to cover so nothing gets overlooked.

- Gap Analysis Forms with sample questions to ask by client type – These forms should ask basic questions that probe your prospects as to their particular challenges.

- Quantification calculation and example sheets – Nothing could be more embarrassing than meeting with a prospect, doing analysis, and then forgetting key calculations that quantify their buying decisions. Always keep a sheet handy that lists the different quantification calculations and how they relate to business. Keep example sheets on hand so prospects can see the kind of quantification calculations you'll be doing.

- Problem and pain list of previous customers – Detail the kinds of challenges other clients have had and how you were able to help them.

- Diagrams of previous customer's buying processes and their titles – This is for the salesperson's reference only and allows him or her to see how the decision making process transpired in other organizations. The salesperson can then have a better chance of approaching the correct people within the current prospect's company.

- Template of first draft proposal, samples of previous first, second, and third draft proposals – Rather than reinventing the wheel with every proposal, it's easier to have a template that you can fill in each time. You may also choose to give a copy of the template to your prospects so they have an idea of what to expect back from you during your presentation.

- List of company people to contact for input regarding product, service, pricing, timing, competition, time to completion of project, etc. – If you get asked questions that you are unable to answer, direct your prospect to someone in your company who can help, or use your list of contacts to research for the prospect's answer yourself.

- Copies of previous successful and unsuccessful proposals including comments as to why the sale was won or lost – This is for the salesperson's reference only. Review past winning and losing proposals so you can determine which aspects worked, which didn't, and why. You can then gear future proposals so they have a higher success rate.

Part Three – Record Keeping and Effort

Finally, keep note of your answers to the following questions in order to determine how many sales you need to meet your goals and to chart your progress.

- How many appointments must you have versus how many did you make?

- How many presentations must you have versus appointments?

- How many first draft proposals must you make versus the number of presentations?

- How many second and third draft proposals must you have in the pipeline versus the number of final proposals made?

- How many sales must you close versus final proposals made?

I followed this process every day from the start-up of my company. After the first 90 days in business, I attended a convention hosted by my franchise company. While there, I met with those people who went through the training at the same time I did. Twenty of us sat around the dinner table the first night to share our first quarter results. I was surprised to learn that of the twelve different companies there, my company outsold every one of them by a very large margin. In fact, we made twice as much money as the next highest company.

When we began to ask questions about why this was, I was shocked to hear that we were the only new company that actually followed the process the franchising company provided. Everyone else drifted from the written process back to either what he or she thought would work or what they used to do in a previous company. In short, they got lazy.

Soon after, we went on to earn recognition for having the "highest gross profit." We even received the "Number One Franchise Award" our third year in business. How did we accomplish this? We simply followed the process day in and day out. Sure, we worked hard and we made the sales calls, but the difference between our super-star achievement and everyone else's was the process. The sales and marketing processes were in place, and we used them to their full potential.

Since then, I have helped develop sales processes for well over 200 different companies. Keep in mind, however, that no two processes are exactly alike, because no two industries or companies are exactly alike. We have developed sales processes for everything from construction companies and manufacturing and job shops to professional organizations and service companies.

In every case where a company did not have an effective selling process, we were able to increase their sales anywhere from 10% to 20% to 50%. I have even documented some at 1000%.

While I have never failed to increase sales with this process, results vary because of local business conditions, competitive pressure, and by type of product or service sold. The only requirements to making the processes work are the desire and effort to make a change, a wholehearted time commitment, quality documentation, a commitment to quantifying each step, and ultimately implementing the processes by the person involved.

Salespeople with proven selling processes will outsell salespeople without selling processes every time. If you can turn the selling project into a process, then you can develop a powerful sales team of two, five, ten, or twenty sales professionals, each one producing higher and higher levels of revenues and profits.

Luckily, setting up sales and marketing processes doesn't cost much to implement. Training and training materials are very low cost, especially when compared to other costs, like computers, people, machinery, or office space. But the best part is the high return on investment. For every dollar invested in sales and marketing processes, it's not unusual to see returns of 100%, 500%, or 1000%, sometimes in as little as 30 to 120 days. Now that's what I call results you can bank on.

It's important to remember that not all business owners are salespeople or have sales skills. So you must be sure you select qualified people with a "sales personality". Training only goes so far if your sales employee does not possess natural sales skills. You must utilize a sales selection process to ensure successful results for your sales force rather than frustration or failure.

Develop Scorecards
Remember, to achieve and sustain success you must measure more than just the short-term finance goals this particular process helps you attain. By developing scorecards and tracking your progress, you can measure

customer satisfaction and the value of processes, meet shareholder needs, discover ways to improve productivity, communicate progress, and create a link to performance bonus and incentive programs.

Scorecards can include goals versus actual, or improvement versus history. The data should focus on critical numbers at a frequency level that makes everyone totally knowledgeable on a timely basis. The idea is to track the progress of a particular process so you can streamline it even further and best utilize it to contribute to your synergy factor.

When you combine your sales and marketing processes with your already established leadership and management processes, you'll create a company that's destined to succeed. You also complete another vital aspect of your company's synergy factor. In the next chapter we'll discuss your operations processes and how they affect your overall profits. You'll discover another piece to the puzzle that will make your business stand out and survive the long term.

Chapter Five

The Third Synergy Factor

"It is not the employer who pays wages - he only handles the money. It is the product that pays wages."
- Henry Ford

The Operations Team Will Get the Job Done On Time, Every Time, at a Profit

Operations vary by industry and company. That's why this chapter is not about the details involved in every industry. As a process practitioner, I will explain what has worked for me and hundreds of my clients over the last thirty years.

Documenting operations processes consists of committed people sitting down together, looking at problems, and documenting and diagramming ways to solve them. This is especially important for the middle manager—the sometimes forgotten person who supervises the shop floor—or the field person who builds the building, makes the products, or services the customer. There are four ideas that must be understood in regards to operational processes:

1. Operations must be output oriented.

2. Teams must be developed.
3. Each manager must have the processes in place to leverage the team.
4. Each step in the process must be standardized and measured.

The Restaurant Job Shop

To better understand the operational process principles, imagine you are a server at a small, local restaurant. Your task is to deliver products in response to the customers' wants, at acceptable quality, within a reasonable time, and at the lowest cost. Operations cannot be held responsible for immediate delivery of whatever the customer wants unless the product is manufactured and inventoried.

In our example, the customer wants a well-done hamburger, hot french fries, and a cold soda. He would like this fairly quickly.

In most small restaurants the expected wait time would be about five to ten minutes from the time the order was placed. In order to document the process, we have to work backwards from our expected completion time. We then list each step in the process along with the time required for each step. This is called process mapping. When analyzing our process map for the hamburger, fries, and soda request, we find the following.

Because the soda is already produced, we can prepare this step in less than a minute. The fries are precut, and take about seven minutes to cook. The hamburger patties are pre-formed, and take about ten minutes to grill, assemble into buns, and place the requested condiments on it. Since the hamburger takes the longest to prepare, the most skill to cook, and is the most important component to the customer, we will organize the entire process around the hamburger. In order to prepare the three components, we must schedule the start and end times of each component to make the process happen.

The key components are time, critical process control, and scheduling. Building a house, manufacturing and distributing a product, or providing a professional or other service contains the exact same components.

Frustrations
The real world, as you know, is filled with barriers and bottlenecks, conditions that cause breakdowns. In our work flow chart, our hamburger meal operation assumes infinite capacity, meaning no one has to wait for an available fryer

or grill. Unfortunately, no such ideal business exists. Think what would happen if you had to wait for an available grill. If you didn't adjust your production flow to account for this change in duration, the fries would get cold and quality control would fail.

This complication can be further worsened by a shortage of staff. If you don't have the trained workers available to do the required tasks, production lags behind. On the other hand, having too many people creates an immense amount of overhead cost.

To eliminate your grill shortage, you could purchase another grill, but this becomes an expensive addition of capital equipment. Another option is to build up a precooked inventory, but that would increase waste.

Because each alternative costs money, the task of the operations processes team is to develop the most cost-effective process and corresponding sub-processes. The key is to optimize resources, including human, material, and equipment. Additionally, if you want to increase profit margins, you need to add value whenever practical. The operational flow of adding value has the same basic characteristics regardless of the industry; the material becomes more valuable as it moves through the process.

For example, a cooked hamburger is more valuable than raw bulk hamburger. A fully assembled meal is more valuable than its component parts. And finally, the meal placed in front of the customer is more valuable still, as it carries the perceived value that the customer associates with the business. Similarly, a finished product or building or service is more valuable than its component parts.

The common rule for developing effective operating and production processes is to focus and fix any problems in the process at the lowest possible cost. Thus, we should find and reject the cold french fries before they are delivered, rather than permitting our customer to find them. The ability to prevent redos and errors, to speed up the process, or to reduce the cost is the difference between the profitability of any two competing organizations.

Indicators and Measurements
Your output is the total number of hamburger meals your restaurant delivers combined with the profits generated and the number of satisfied customers. The number of possible indicators is limitless, but to be useful they must be applied on a specific operational goal and process.

Let's say you're the manager of "Joe's Hamburgers." To develop your operational process, you will work with five indicators to meet your production goals on a daily basis.

1. First you want a sales forecast. How many hamburger meals should you plan to deliver on a daily basis? Forecasting is a separate process.

2. Your next indicator would be raw materials inventory. Do you have enough soft drink syrup, potatoes, hamburgers, and buns? If not, you'll have to order more. If you have too much, you may want to cancel today's order.

3. Another component is your equipment. If anything is broken, it must be repaired.

4. You must also forecast your manpower. Do you have enough help to get each job done? Or do you have too many people who don't have enough work to keep them busy?

5. Finally, you need a customer satisfaction indicator to make sure you never lose your market appeal.

All these indicators are essential. What gets measured gets done. That means that any measurement is more important than no measurement.

A great indicator focuses on results, not activity. For example:

Operating Function	*Output Indicator*
Potato production	Number of pounds of potatoes
Hamburger production	Number of grilled and assembled sandwiches delivered
Plant operations	Number of total jobs delivered
Administrative operations	Number of invoices processed
Human resources	Number of people recruited and trained

This process can be turned into a game to help increase performance along with having fun and building teams.

The Black Box

Think of "Joe's Hamburgers" restaurant as if it were a black box. Whatever you input into the box has a direct impact on the results the box produces. Similarly, we can draw a black box to represent a job shop, a construction company, or a professional service business.

The input could be lumber and nails, or steel and wood, or forms and reports. The labor is the work of the technical and management team, and the output includes buildings built, parts manufactured, patients seen, tax forms processed, or whatever the end result that your business produces.

By peering into our black box we can get a clearer picture of what indicators need to be developed and monitored to increase profits. There are operating indicators and process indicators. Examples include productivity and labor, hours per unit of sale, cost per unit, sales forecast versus actual, product units manufactured versus plan, cost per unit of output, employee turnover, and so forth.

The idea is to work smarter, not harder. The best way to think of this concept is leverage. If we can get people to speed up without losing quality, we can leverage our current process to an even higher level. Automation is one way to do this.

A second method to leverage existing resources is called work simplification. To make this work, you must first create a process map of the operating process as it exists today. No step can be left out. Then, count the number of steps in the process map so you know how many you started with. Set a target for a reduction in the number of steps. Shoot for at least 30%. The way to do this is to ask questions about each step. Can certain steps be combined, automated, shortened, outsourced, etc.? When you leverage your resources, you create high performance operating departments that focus on reducing output costs and increasing profit margins.

Customer Satisfaction

When your operating processes are running smoothly, your customers will be satisfied with the product or services they rely on you for. The fact is, no business can survive long without total customer satisfaction. Customers quit buying when they are not satisfied. As a result, prices cannot be increased. Referrals stop so sales decline. Invoices stop being paid, and lawsuits begin all because of poor customer satisfaction.

Customer dissatisfaction occurs when a customer perceives that a promise was not kept. Promises may include quality of work, speed of work, adhering to deadlines, and customer service.

Companies generally don't keep their promises because of one or more of the following reasons:

1. The company lacks a clear up front sales contract.

2. The company lacks an effective production, delivery, or customer service strategy.

3. The company lacks the trained, quality people to implement the processes.

Additionally a failure to constantly communicate causes customers to feel that employees don't care or are simply not on top of things.

What Customer Dissatisfaction and Failed Operations Cost

I have consulted six successful construction companies, all of which have been in business for over twenty years. Regardless of the fact that they have many years of experience and good people, every one of these six companies had very costly customer satisfaction problems. The costs of these problems averaged from $5,000 to $30,000 per incident. I have personally seen problems cost over $200,000.

This expense comes directly out of profits. Even worse, these problems occur several times per year, year after year. The resulting costs represent only the dollars lost; they don't include the impact an unsatisfied customer has on future business or how upset employees can drain morale and affect sales.

The story is the same in nearly every industry, with manufacturing redos, errors, production problems, or bottlenecks in the workflow, all of which result in thousands of lost dollars. I have worked with over 15 manufacturers, and in every case there has been errors and production problems costing 10, 20 even 30% of sales.

Service businesses are equally problematic. Medical, legal, accounting, ad agencies, insurance, and training businesses fail to keep customers 80% of the time due to customer dissatisfaction. Patients and clients wait too long for service, they are treated rudely, and they are not listened to. As a result, they go somewhere else, costing thousands of dollars year after year while business owners and managers continue to make excuses, such as "We didn't have enough time," "We didn't have enough trained people," or "We didn't know about the problems." If not corrected, this arrogant attitude takes the business down eventually.

The solution to 90% of all customer satisfaction and operational problems lies in developing a gap analysis, which is driven by an up front sales agreement. The next step is to develop effective service, production, and capacity planning processes. Finally, someone needs to be reporting the quantification of each process to ensure it's working effectively. The result will be jobs that are done on time, every time, exactly as promised.

Every business's operations department has four major functions:

1. Product or services specifications.

2. Production process.

3. Delivery process.

4. Customer service.

These four parts include design, prototype, manufacturing, constructing assembly, quality control, and vendor selection, just to name a few. It involves building the building and manufacturing the parts. It's what you do. The keys to effective client fulfillment are work flow, quality, and cost control. It means getting the best result for the least cost while creating a loyal customer in the process.

Operations must develop all the processes necessary to give the customers what the sales team promised and what they perceive to be expected. Operations is the core—the heart of the business. So operations requires the time and the best thinking in order to give the customers exactly what they want on time, every time, exactly as promised. It's the never-ending process of reaching for perfection.

Develop Scorecards
Once again, to achieve and sustain success you must measure more than just the short-term finance goals this particular process helps you attain. By developing

scorecards and tracking your progress, you can measure customer satisfaction and the value of processes, meet shareholder needs, discover ways to improve productivity, communicate progress, and create a link to performance bonus and incentive programs.

Scorecards can include goals versus actual, or improvement versus history. The data should focus on critical numbers at a frequency level that makes everyone totally knowledgeable on a timely basis. The idea is to track the progress of a particular process so you can streamline it even further and best utilize it to contribute to your synergy factor.

You now have another piece of your company's synergy factor. All the synergies we've discussed so far lead up to the one synergy that matters most to business owners and managers: Financial. Without the necessary profits, no business can grow. So let's continue with our final process to complete the Synergy Factor.

Chapter Six

The Fourth Synergy Factor

The Finance and Information Team

"Profitability is the sovereign criterion of the enterprise."
— *Peter Drucker*

Why 80% of All Businesses Fail to Make Enough Cash to Keep the Doors Open: A Lack of Financial Synergy is Key.
Profits are and always will be the number one concern of every owner and manager. In order to create and accurately track profits, several components must be in place, including budgets, profit plans, growth plans to obtain increased financial capabilities, cash flow plans, document control, conversion cycle of assets (turnover), terms of sales, accounts receivables, accounts payables, job profit analysis, product/service profit analysis, and personnel cost ratios, just to name a few. Understanding where profits and cash flow are coming from or not coming from is the purpose of having financial processes in place.

Happiness in business means having a positive cash flow. One of the main reasons for business failure is running out of cash. The challenge is that cash flow is not always easy to read. The first step to understanding cash flow is to set a cash flow objective for the month and year-end. Cash flow problems can often be avoided by developing a cash flow planning process, which includes the budget process, the accounts receivable process, and the work in progress process.

Realize that with every job, time delays have a cost. Jobs that drag on can create cash flow problems because they delay invoices going out on time and keep you from collecting your money fast enough. Additionally, when you don't get advance deposits for every job, you slow your payables (using credit cards can help reduce immediate cash outlays). Inventory control processes can be critical as well. Excessive inventory or its mismanagement can cripple your cash flow.

Pricing processes are also critical to profit and maintaining a positive cash flow. Increased competition has put pressure on pricing, so simply raising prices to earn extra money won't work in today's business climate. That's why profits and profit plans are a critical priority.

Successful business owners know they must manage customers for profits as well as sales. High sales volume does not necessarily mean high income, as many business owners have learned to their sorrow. It costs more to fill some orders than others; therefore, your pricing must reflect that difference. Too many owners and managers pay little attention to customer profitability. They give in to large accounts, as these accounts demand higher and higher discounts, more service, and longer terms, only to discover they have eroded profits and end up with losses. I have seen these same businesses raise prices to the so-called "worthless" accounts. While these small customers initially seem to be more trouble than they're worth, the business owner ends up discovering that they actually made more money and received higher profits from these small customer orders.

Without a good cost accounting process there is no way a business can understand order, product, customer, or market segment profitability. Developing a pricing strategy includes shifting or changing the product, the customer group, the distribution channel, or the sales strategy. A business's ability to raise pricing depends on the customers' perceived value of the product or service versus their perceived value of the competitions' product or service. Part of the perceived value includes the uniqueness of the product or the numbers of suppliers bidding on a typical order. Pricing is also an important component of the marketing function, as the more successfully you can market the product, the more you can ask for it.

The Lack of The Synergy Factor Can Drain Your Profits

While owners and managers believe they are paying attention to the most important expenses, it's usually necessary for them to look deeper. They must focus instead on errors, ineffective processes, redos, low productivity, poor allocation of resources, slow capitol turnover, and old technology that is causing gaps. Most companies fail to identify and then to correct these problems fast enough.

Undetected financial errors routinely occur when employees and managers fail to fill out company forms completely or correctly. These kinds of errors cost businesses thousands of dollars in lost profits each year.

Ineffective processes occur when companies fail to take the time to document and measure the correct way to do an important key financial process. The lack of effective financial processes costs most companies thousands of dollars in lost profits each year. Specifically, a study by G.E. has proven that many businesses are spending somewhere between 10% and 40% of profits on redo work alone. This is the subject of Six Sigma, a business process that focuses on redos as the biggest single killer of a business's profits.

People can work very hard and believe they are doing things well enough, but my experience has proven this thinking to be a fatal flaw. In fact, the major cause for lost profits is that the owners and managers are too busy working *in* one or more jobs rather than *with* the teams and the process maps to correct these profit killing problems. Additionally, most owners and managers don't know what to do because they simply haven't seen a better way.

However, all the processes we've talked about to this point have a direct impact on the financial result of a business. For example:

- If sales don't increase, profits can't increase.

- If management can't keep, recruit, and train increasing numbers of quality people, profits can't increase.

- If operations doesn't create a satisfied customer, profits can't increase.

Below are the 10 main reasons for profit decline. Management's job is to focus on creating and measuring all the necessary processes required to change each of the reasons listed.

10 Main Reasons for Profit Decline

1. Don't control costs, including redos and errors.

2. Disregard or misinterpret financial data and fail to share this information.

3. Keep inadequate records, especially regarding time and material costs of critical jobs.

4. Fail to market aggressively.

5. Lack of proper strategic planning.

6. Fail to develop processes to improve results.

7. Fail to have an effective human resources strategy, including recruiting, selecting, incentives, mentoring, and training employees.

8. Have insufficient working capital.

9. Do not seek experienced help when necessary.

10. Place blame towards others rather than create a process to stop any pattern of errors from recurring.

How Financial Synergy Helps Increase Profits

The purpose of finance and accounting processes is to make sure a percentage of the money coming in is reinvested in income producing assets. Today, because of the tremendous move toward services and the value of trained productive people, we would include people as the most important asset. Other income producing assets include trucks, special equipment, computers, machinery, and so forth. Additionally functional areas such as marketing and advertising, new product development, and training are income-producing assets. Stocks in other companies, bonds and money markets, and real estate are also income producing assets.

The idea is to move money into those assets that will give the company the best returns. Returns should be planned for both the short term and the long term of the business. On the contrary, funding should be reduced or even eliminated to those assets that are not producing. In other words, people who produce the most should be paid the most, functional departments that produce the most should receive the most, and so forth. Needless to say, all critical functions and processes necessary to the business's success must receive adequate money allocation.

The purpose is to move more money to areas that will bring the greatest return over the long run. To illustrate this point, I've watched as finance and accounting people recommend that a business cut back on their marketing and advertising budgets when business revenues drop. However, if advertising and public relations has proven it can supply a constant stream of quality leads to the sales department, cutting their funds might save money for a short period, but in the long term, the results of that decision could actually threaten the future revenues of the business, causing catastrophic loses.

This same kind of analysis can be applied to any function in the company. The idea is for the finance and accounting processes to do more than just supply profit and loss statements and balance sheets, which is nothing more than history. The idea is to supply management with functional information reports that show results based on trends that look favorable for the future. By changing the way you think about these finance and administrative functions, the more valuable this department becomes.

If your business's profits are not what you'd like them to be, there are ways to give them a boost. Below are the 10 best ways that any company can increase profits.

10 Rules to Increase Profits
1. Create a strategic plan for growing your business. Establish indicators to measure performance and develop processes to hold people accountable for the numbers.

2. Throw out the old management model you started your business with and start a new one. Innovation is the key to beating the competition.

3. Develop an operational and financial reporting process that allows you to track all your critical numbers. What gets measured, gets done.

4. Identify all the key people who are driving your company and create incentives for them to grow.

5. Hold daily or weekly mentoring and team meetings to go over the numbers and make adjustments to action plans.

6. Every business owner and manager must make a personal transformation and commitment to working on the business, not just in the business. They must develop the processes and people to reduce and eliminate problems.

7. Develop a business growth attitude that drives the numbers higher today and even higher tomorrow.

8. You must transform the business from an ownership model to a process driven model.

9. You must transform from an "emotional" decision-maker to a "fact-based" decision-maker.

10. You must focus on the fact that the key to success in business is to gather information, weigh costs versus benefits, and manage by numbers not feelings.

Notice that none of these suggestions are one-time quick-fix ideas. They are all suggestions that need to become permanent changes for your business. When you try to solve your cash flow problems with a "bandage" approach, you only temporarily fix the problem. While your cash flow or profits may initially improve, it's only a matter of time before you're right back where you started. When you commit to making positive, long-term changes to your business model, your improvements will be ongoing, and your profits will positively reflect your new business direction.

Develop Scorecards
As with all the previous processes, to achieve and sustain success you must measure more than just the short-term finance goals this particular process helps you attain. By developing scorecards and tracking your progress, you can measure customer satisfaction and the value of processes, meet shareholder needs, discover ways to improve productivity, communicate progress, and create a link to performance bonus and incentive programs.

Scorecards can include goals versus actual, or improvement versus history. The data should focus on critical numbers at a frequency level that makes everyone totally knowledgeable on a timely basis. The idea is to track the progress of a particular process so you can streamline it even further and best utilize it to contribute to your synergy factor.

With the proper financial processes in place, you're one step closer to completing your company's synergy factor. When you combine your financial processes with the previous three processes, your business is ready to reach new levels of success. But as with any new endeavor, you can't do it all alone. That's why it's necessary to train your employees on the proper process implementation. Next we'll discuss why employee training is so important to your business's profitability and long-term growth.

Chapter Seven

The Fifth Synergy Factor

Scorecards

"To solve a problem it is necessary to think. It is necessary to think even to decide what facts to collect."
- *Robert Maynard Hutchins*

Most businesses would like more accountability and most people would be more open to accountability if they knew it was fair and they had some control. If you add fun and rewards in the process you would create a game.

If you could add the challenge and the fun of playing a game in the work people did in the business you would have a higher motivated workforce.

If you selected the right people, created a powerful strategic plan, developed the processes that work and then add the fun and accountability of scorecards the Synergy Factor would be in full force in your business.

Business owners and managers are deluged daily with reports, paperwork, e-mail and meetings but many times still can't tell if they're really winning or losing. That's because they have less time today to analyze, decipher, interpret and act on the best right decision faster because they only have those indicators necessary to look at.

Starting with your strategic plan then moving through each function's plans, i.e.; marketing, advertising, sales, operations, management and finance - you and your management team create scorecards determined by key result areas. Example of items to score include customer loyalty, advertising leads, quality of leads, operational effectiveness, employee development and financial success, to name a few. As you develop your first scorecards don't be concerned that they are going to be perfect because they won't be. As you test your new scorecards you will learn to fine-tune them to identify and execute improvements. Scorecards help employees see results and help clear up work processes. When people can see the numbers they better understand what needs to be done instead of being told. This results in both an improvement of performance as well as improvement of relationships.

Performance scorecards reduce conflict and speed up progress because they focus only on those few key measurements each person or team is responsible for. Huge amounts of time are saved by eliminating irrelevant information. By linking scorecards by department your company achieves a tremendous productivity advantage which drives up profits and cash flow, motivates people while holding them accountable. Scorecard design starts with the budget goal, customer requirements, core processes, and department objectives.

At the top of the organization the key management team will develop scorecards for sales, gross margins, expense control, net profit, cash flow, stock value, new product development and customer loyalty.

The marketing and advertising function will score new customer inquiries, media costs versus leads generated, market share increases, etc. The sales function will score number of leads, quality of leads, number of contacts made, number of presentations, number of estimates, number of quality leads in the pipeline and dollar and profit amount of sales closed.

The operations department will score quality of products, number of errors, number of redos, costs, productivity, output, capacity, etc.

The finance department will score profit and loss, balance sheets, ratios, cash flow, budget variance, capital turnover, cost of capital, industry benchmarks, etc.

Human Resources will score effectiveness of recruiting, selecting, retaining, training, rewarding, healthcare, insurance, safety, etc.

The scorecards will be modified as they move through the organizations to better measure objectives closest to each position and team's key result area. As you gain experience in scorecards you will have historical data versus target goal data. This will enable management to execute improvements through actions based on very specific results. Improved performance reviews and process requirements will be apparent to everyone.

Case Study:
See Construction Company's (not their real name; see case study in chapter nine) top strategic goal was to increase profits by 10% by year end. The marketing and advertising scorecard focused on increasing leads by 10% and a budget of 6%.

The sales scorecard focused on increasing their closing rate by 10% on those products and service that yielded a gross margin of 60% or more.

The operation's scorecard focused on a 10% reduction in costs by reducing redos and errors by 30%.

The human resources' and manager's scorecards focused on increasing productivity by 10% through selecting, training and retaining people.

The finance scorecard focused on a 10% reduction in interest and cost of capital by benchmarking at least 3 new sources of capital and increasing collections by 20%.

The CEO scorecard consisted of the above scorecard summaries and the performance, strategy and process improvements achieved in any scorecard that was failing to reach its objective.

See Construction's actual result at year end was a 35% increase in profits. It doesn't take a genius to see why. (No pun intended)

From Scorecard to Incentives

The bottom line of scorecard incentives is to educate the employees about business. Employees are trained to understand the key result areas. They must know sales, cost of sales and gross profits. They must know overhead expenses, wages, health care costs, tax increases and other costs.

They must understand the difference between revenues and profits. They must know how each department, team and individual affects the profits. Once everyone understands the numbers and how they and the processes effect them the business changes for the better.

Once people know the costs of time, materials and redos, they begin to understand how to make changes for improvement. An educated workforce will beat an uneducated workforce every day of the week.

Teaching employees process mapping and finance and allowing them to have input into developing improvements gives them the highest level of accountability - trust and team spirit. When they understand the numbers and how to improve them; bonus and involvement drive and motivate the people. A motivated workforce will beat an unmotivated workforce every day of the week.

The problem with educating the workforce is that no two people have exactly the same level of knowledge. Training must be made simple enough to make it easy for everyone.

If you can turn your business into a game and you can teach people how to score, you can create a scorecard for every team and person. If they can develop processes to improve, the company shares with them through bonuses. The more profit they generate, the bigger the bonuses. It's a way to give people more money without jeopardizing profit and cash flow.

Why do Bonus Programs Fail?
The number one reason is the people didn't know what they could do to achieve goals.

Divide people into teams. Develop two or three objectives. For example, the #1 goal might be operating profit, #2 is gross margin. Train everyone in process mapping and finance, and most importantly, make it fun. The way you do this is to turn the business into a game and the financials are a part of the scorecards. Next, you put a functional team on every line on the income statement.

Incentives

You can generate more income by sharing. That's because a company that pays for performance will out-perform a company that doesn't any day of the week.

Look what Bill Gates created. MicroSoft's secret to success is having one of the most motivated workforces on earth. MicroSoft keeps people motivated with stock. This is a great opportunity available to most businesses. Especially to start a buy-out process or ESOP.

You may not solve all of your problems. But you will gain more control by getting people to think about process improvement. You make it possible for people to understand how to operate at peak performance. Performance improvement is the only control people really have. As long as people perform, do what they promise and add value, your sales and profits will increase. Scorecards help you to do all that and have fun in the process.

Developing the Game

Everything must be simple and easy to understand for every employee. If we use football as a common game, a comparative to our business, it's easier for people to understand. For example, there are four quarters in a football game and you have four quarters in your business plan. In football, you have four tries to get 10 yards and in your business you have 4 weeks to achieve your monthly goal. In football, you have offense, defense and starters and in business you have marketing and sales, operations and finance. In football, the objective is to win 12 games out of 15 to reach the play-offs. In business, the objective is to hit 9 months out of 12 to reach bonus territory. Divisional championship is 1st bonus level. League championship is 2nd bonus level. Super Bowl is 3rd level, and winner of Super Bowl is 4th level.

If you beat the numbers at year end, the bonus increases, managers and master craftsmen get 15% - 20%, and all others get up to 5% - 15% of their base wage. You must work through the numbers to make it work for your business.

The Scorecard

The statistics for the game may include:

    Sales
    COG's
    Gross Profit
    Subcontracted Costs
    Expenses
    Interest
    Net Profit
    Cash

Ratios might include:
    Debt to Equity
    (ROS) Return on Sales
    (ROA) Return on Assets
    Quick Ratio
    Current Assets vs Current Liabilities

Operating Ratios might include:
    P/R to Sales
    O/H Absorption Rates

Marketing and Sales Ratios might include:
    Leads Generated
    Leads Converted to Estimates
    Estimates Converted to Sales
    Number of New Clients
    Gross Profits of New Clients

Select the critical numbers and develop your own customized P/L. This becomes the scoreboard. Set a minimum and maximum payout of profits. Develop a payout for people based on a percent of their base pay. Keep it simple.

Part III

Chapter Eight

The Biggest Advantage Any Business Can Have is an Educated, Trained Workforce

"Sixty years ago I knew everything; now I know nothing; education is a progressive discovery of our own ignorance."
                                                                -Will Durant

A key component to process mapping is educating and training your employees on how the processes work. Unfortunately, many business owners miss this concept. After developing the necessary processes, they mistakenly keep the knowledge to themselves or share it with just a few key managers. They neglect to teach their business processes to the most important people of all: those who are actually doing the work and who must rely on those processes to get the job done.

The biggest advantage any business can attain is having the best educated and trained workforce. Truth be known, most services and products are more similar than dissimilar. Sure, your product may come in different colors than your competitor's, or your service may have a slightly different spin, but on the whole, everyone has basically the same tools and equipment. Therefore, what separates companies apart are the employees and how they implement their service and product knowledge.

In most businesses, education and training are separated into two categories: technical and managerial. Technical includes skilled trades, sales, finance, engineering, medical, computers, and so forth. The focus of technical education and training is on how to get the work done.

On the other hand, management education and training focuses on goals, organization, motivation, planning, measuring, hiring, documenting processes, innovation, research, and everything to do with obtaining results through people.

Successful companies budget for education and training costs. They plan regularly scheduled time and resources to get the job done. When a new employee is hired, they are immediately educated and trained in the methods and processes the business has established. If you think about it, education and training just makes good common sense; yet most small businesses simply don't do it.

Those companies that do attempt to educate and train new workers routinely fail to allocate enough time, or the training is not orchestrated for a desired result or improvement. Based on my experience, lack of training is the second leading reason for failure to improve sales, quality, profit, and cash flow.

Many small business owners rely on the workers to train themselves or believe the skills acquired at previous jobs constitute training. In fact, most small businesses hire an outsider whom they believe has the experience necessary to perform the job. In the case where a person has been promoted from within, the company believes the newly promoted person will do things the way he or she has been, yet with an expected improvement. The end result in both cases is usually not good.

Let me explain why. If you are relatively successful and have been in business five years or more, chances are you got that way because of the way you did things. A new employee comes aboard with experience learned from another company. The new employee may even say, "This is the way we did it at my old company." The new employee then proceeds to do the job as his or her previous employer did. This almost always fails simply because you are not the other company.

To make matters worse, you pay the new person more money, only to discover it will take a year for the new hire to return to your company an improved result. And in some instances, they never do. This is not to say that a new hire never makes a dramatic contribution to the bottom line, because sometimes it's possible. Every situation is different. In either case education and training can only improve the situation.

The best way to alleviate this problem is to train your new employees or newly promoted employees in your processes from day one. The best training is hands-on, so simply relying on a manual or other pre-printed materials usually doesn't work. Identify one key person per department who is exceptional at training and allow the new hire to shadow that person during the training process. Make it clear to the new person why the processes were developed, how they work, how to perform them, and how to track results. Training is simply the only way to expect a new hire to get up to speed in a reasonable amount of time.

Management Training is Vital As Well

Workers who perform well are usually selected for management positions. Many times an excellent worker takes the promotion simply because it pays more. This is a huge mistake. Only offer management positions to those employees who enjoy people and who know how to get work done through others. Next, train each new manager as if he or she is a new hire.

The majority of managers who fail do so, because they were never educated and trained in management skills. They don't know how to lead and develop their employees. They approach their new position with a worker's mentality. They're still focusing on the task, not the overall result. Great managers are more motivated by the results of their employees than by their own success. Lack of manager training is a huge mistake, because when managers fail, business fails. It's that simple.

How The Synergy Factor Increases Profits and Growth

When processes are in place and the employees are trained in their development and implementation, a growth and profit cycle will begin to develop. Here's a typical example:

1. When you take the time to write out exactly what the customer expects, a sales estimate, and an agreement process including standards, time frames,

and cost, both the customer and the company benefit by knowing up front the exact job specifications.

2. When workers have all the operating processes written and are trained in their use, they get the job done on time, exactly at the standards the customers expect.

3. When customers have a positive experience, they make another purchase and then another. As long as they get the same results each time, they won't leave and they'll refer others to you.

To calculate the value of creating the processes involved, you would first have to calculate the lifetime value of a customer's average sale, multiplied by the average frequency of purchase, multiplied by the number of months or years you retain them as customers. Second, you calculate the value of new sales created through referrals and word of mouth. Then you add up the totals multiplied by the number of customers you want to keep.

For example, if the average sale is $2,000 and the frequency is 12 times per year, that equals $24,000. If the average customer lasts three years, then $24,000 multiplied by three equals $72,000. And if the operating margin is 80%, $72,000 multiplied by 80% equals $57,600.

If the average customer gave you one referral, then you would add another $57,600. So the total value in this case equals $115,200 return for the time and money you spent learning to create innovative processes. This doesn't include the time spent on additional profits made through the reduction of errors and redos.

Synergy Factor Training Reduces Cycle Times

We define cycle time as how long it takes from the time you get the sale until the time you close the project and collect the money. We know the faster you can do that, the more you can increase your cash flow and profits. The processes required to achieve this include Project Processes, Organizational Strategy, Job Descriptions, Time Management, Mentoring, and Scheduling Calendar, just to name a few. When people know in writing who, what, when, how, and why in detailed process maps, everything speeds up dramatically.

If the average project is $20,000 and operating profit is 80%, then the current cycle operating profit or contribution is $16,000. For example, if it takes two months on average to do six projects, you multiply that by $16,000 and get a $96,000 profit margin. If you take the time to develop the processes and train the employees, you could reduce that cycle time from two months to one month. By doing that, your profits would double in the first year. In this case, instead of an operating profit of $96,000 it would increase to $192,000.

Synergy Factor Training Increases Employee Motivation

Motivated people out-produce unmotivated people any day of the week. Not only do they produce more, but they also do the job better, faster, and without waste. Employees aren't motivated by accident. Motivation requires a clear understanding of the goals and the rewards for achieving them.

The processes required for motivation include the ability to find what people want up-front and the means to show them a plan to attain those goals. A few of the processes would be Personal Goals, Job Descriptions, Personality and Ability Testing, Problem Solving Tools, Process Mapping, and Skills Training. While it's difficult to project value here, profit increases of 10% to 30% are common and are conservative estimates.

The real excitement begins when you start to combine these processes and strategies. You add the value of not losing a customer plus the value of increasing cycle times to the value of increasing motivation. When you do that, it's not difficult to prove profit increases of 10% to 100% and more. I personally have case studies of over 1000% increases in net profit in less than one year.

If the average process training runs $1,600 to $4,900 a month, you should forecast operating profit increases that pay the cost plus increase profits by 10%, 20%, 30% or more, depending on what and how you're doing things now plus how committed you are to improving your situation. Since every company is different, every result is different. You need to develop profit improvement objectives up-front in order to understand the value you receive from the training.

Synergy Factor Training Increases Your Company's Velocity

Velocity is the most under appreciated component of return on investment. For most finance managers, it's not even on the radar screen. However, those who grasped the importance of velocity have built fortunes.

Here's a classic example. In the 1950s Arthur Wood, Chairman of the Board of Sears, the world's largest retailer, told the North Western College School of Management, "There is no growth in retailing." At the same time this was happening, Sam Walton, founder of Wal-Mart, was building a retail empire like the world had never seen. He lowered margins by increased inventory turnover and by capturing quantifying information. This is velocity at its greatest.

Over the years, research has revealed nine sources of business growth:

1. Capitalizing on market demand when the market is strong for what you're selling.

2. Gaining market share through low cost, high productivity rapid cycle times and high asset turnover.

3. Developing proprietary or patent technology.

4. Having highly developed distribution channels.

5. Creating new markets for existing products.

6. Participating in acquisitions, alliances, and vertical integrations.

7. Expanding your product line.

8. Re-segmenting your markets.

9. Moving into adjacent markets.

All paths to this growth lie in one of four quadrants:

1. Existing customers with existing needs.

2. New customers with existing needs.

3. New customers with new needs.

4. Existing customers with new needs.

Somebody may already be supplying the solution to the need, but it usually can be satisfied by more than one product. Could that product be yours? Or, can you create a new need your current products will fill? Needs are always changing. In these instances, creativity, judgment, and training pay off. Some of the common pay-offs are:

(M) Margin   =   (V) Velocity

Annual productivity improvements = Faster inventory or job turnover

Faster time to market = Lower capital investment per dollar of sales

New products and services = Reduced working capital

Creative segmentation markets = Additional sales from the assets

The answer to profit margin and velocity improvement lies in strategic planning, innovation, quantification and training. There must be constant productivity improvement, new products, new markets, and new channels. Even more important, for all the factors to work together, employees must be trained in every aspect that applies to them. This is a huge factor to business growth and beating the competition. The battle never ends.

The Power of Training and Speed Learning

Wealth and power in the last 200-500 years have been in natural resources, i.e.: oil, coal, and land. Wealth and power in the last hundred years have been in technology, i.e.: electronics, pharmaceutical, computers, software, etc. Wealth and power now are in people and how fast they can learn a better process technology.

This is not new thinking. In 1890 Andrew Carnegie, the richest man in the world and the founder of U.S. Steel, would only hire immigrants. Most people thought he did so because they were cheap labor. Wrong. He hired immigrants because they were eager to learn new things and he could train them to do things in processes that had proven to be productive. As a result, U.S. Steel could undersell the competition because their processes were 50% more productive. If you can find a proven better process, you can teach people to use it much faster than if you tried to reinvent it.

Another way to analyze training and speed learning is to compare it with new technology, like computers. When making an ROI decision on computers, you normally measure the increased productivity the computer will enable you to achieve (reduced cost calculated versus cost of money invested). A second calculation is the estimated payback time. For example, if you invest $25,000 in new hardware and $15,000 in software, how long would it take to pay back the $40,000 investment? Many times, these calculations are off dramatically. The reason technology investments take longer than estimated to get paid back is that most managers forget he rule of thumb, which is every dollar invested in hardware will cost $100 in employee training. A second important fact usually missing is that a dollar improvement today is usually worth more than a dollar in the future.

The Synergy Factor happens when the combined effect of new technology and trained people peak. An investment today brings far greater returns over time. This same calculation holds true for innovated, measured process improvement and trained teams.

Assess Your Training Needs
Marketing, advertising and public relations, sales, finance, and operating managers are required to increase the performance of their departments, because if all the parts succeed then so will the whole. To determine where education and training is needed, analyze each department's results. Those that are lagging need more process training.

If sales aren't where they should be, then education and training in marketing, advertising and public relations, and sales should be a top priority. If products and services are not getting done on time, at a profit, and with 100% customer satisfaction, then operations should be considered for process education and training, and so on throughout the organization. Performance goals versus baseline should be developed, and education and training goals should be benchmarked against them. In the end this will prove its value or lack thereof.

Some owners/managers may complain that training is a waste because of turnover; however, it's probably better to train your employees and lose them rather than not train them and keep them. A trained workforce will out produce an untrained workforce any day of the week.

Develop Scorecards
Training, too, requires scorecards. To achieve and sustain success you must measure more than just the short-term finance goals this particular process helps you attain. By developing scorecards and tracking your progress, you can measure customer satisfaction and the value of processes, meet shareholder needs, discover ways to improve

productivity, communicate progress, and create a link to performance bonus and incentive programs.

Scorecards can include goals versus actual, or improvement versus history. The data should focus on critical numbers at a frequency level that makes everyone totally knowledgeable on a timely basis. The idea is to track the progress of a particular process so you can streamline it even further and best utilize it to contribute to your synergy factor.

The bottom line is that if you take the time to develop the various processes, you must also take the time to train your employees on their implementation. Without the process knowledge spread throughout the organization, the process itself is useless, and your company can't grow. When you combine all the processes with adequate training, you complete your company's synergy factor.

Chapter Nine

A Typical Business

"My greatest strength as a consultant is to be ignorant and ask a few questions."

- Peter Drucker

I pull into the parking lot of See Construction at 8:15 a.m. This is my first appointment with the owners of this family-owned and operated business. As I walk in the front door and enter a small reception area, I immediately notice the clutter of boxes filled with magazines and scrap parts. A busy receptionist opens a small glass-sliding window while she is simultaneously answering an unending series of in-coming calls. I write the owner's name on my card and slip it through the window. The receptionist looks at the card, nods her head, and slides the window closed. It's obvious that either she doesn't have enough help or that she lacks a process to help her do everything she's responsible for.

After a few minutes, a smiling woman comes through the inner office door and reaches her hand out to me. "Hi, I'm Sharon See," she says. "You must be Gary."

"Yes," I reply as I shake her hand.

"Come on back," she says as she turns and heads into the office area. As I follow her, I see more and more clutter and people working feverishly processing paper, working project problems, trying to train new workers, answering phones, etc. We enter a small office. A man, about Sharon's age with a deep frown, looks at me. "This is my husband Bill See," she says.

I introduce myself and sit in a chair in front of his desk. After a few minutes of small talk, Bill asks why I'm here.

"Well," I reply, "your wife responded to a letter I sent a few weeks ago. It outlined our training services and contained some information about how we help businesses develop the processes necessary to set clear goals, organize the work, measure everyone's productivity, and help develop high performance teams. We call it The Synergy Factor. The result is an organization that runs as smoothly as a Fortune 500 company, say like the Ford Motor Company."

"That sounds great," he says. "But we're not a car manufacturer, nor are we a Fortune 500 company. We're a construction company. And besides, we don't want to become that big. Sure, we want to grow, but our business plan doesn't include becoming a world giant with offices and plants worldwide"

"Bill," I reply, "When Ford started making cars, they didn't look at themselves as just another car manufacturer. They looked at themselves as a growing business. And the way a small business gets to be a bigger business, at some point, is it begins to act like a bigger business. The major difference between a small business's strategy and a bigger business's strategy is in the balance of people, time, and resources toward the critical functions needed. This includes Leadership and Management, Sales and Marketing, Operations, and Finance. When Ford began growing, the owners began looking at what they needed to do *as a business* rather than just the technical operations of the business. That's why they took the time to document every important detail from how to hire and assemble the products to how to market and develop effective financial and cash control reports. As a result, they had the resources to grow and continue the business for generations. Isn't that what you and your wife want? Didn't you start this business because you wanted the opportunity to make more money, do something you enjoy, and develop financial and personal freedom?"

"Are you kidding?" Bill responds. "First of all, I can't predict what my sales will be, so either we're too busy or not busy enough. And there are too many problems for me to get time off. Why, I haven't had a two week vacation in 15 years."

From the hallway I hear someone calling, "Mr. See." Just then a guy sticks his head in. It's one of his foremen. "Hey, Bill," the foreman says, "you better come out here. We've got a real problem on the Smith project, and Joan and John are arguing again about not having the trained people we need." The foreman doesn't even wait for Bill to answer. He just turns and walks away.

"Look, Gary, I have to fix another damn problem." He turns to his wife. "Sharon, why don't you show Gary around the office and the sales department." With that, Bill bolts out the door and out of sight.

"Come, Gary," Sharon says. "Let me show you around." As we pass various desks, Sharon introduces me to each employee. Most of them are trying to work on cluttered desks, and there are boxes and piles everywhere.

"Here's our sales and estimating department," Sharon says as we walk through an office door where several pictures of buildings they completed are on the wall. "This is Chris, our sales manager."

We both say "hi" almost simultaneously. Chris is a friendly, outgoing person who seems full of enthusiasm. Chris begins to explain how the sales department works.
"So, how are sales?" I ask.

"Well, we were growing over 15% in the past, but now sales are growing at only 5%."

"What do you think is the cause?" I ask.

Sharon jumps in, "I'm not sure if it's our price or the economy or the additional competition. We're doing some advertising and trade shows and getting some new estimates, but it's just not like it used to be."

Just then, Chris' phone rings and I can tell by the discussion that it is a customer complaint. We sneak out the door to leave Chris to calm down an unhappy client.

"Bill's most likely going to be tied up for a while," says Sharon. "Do you think you can help us break out of this rut, Gary? We want to retire in five years and sell out to the employees. If we can do that, our long time employees can have ownership, and it will supply us with income for our retirement. Plus, we'd like the business to continue if it can. After all, we put twenty years into it and we'd hate to see all that hard work go down the tubes."

"Sharon, if you can give me three years of P&Ls, I will go back to my office and do an analysis based on the notes I've taken this morning and a review of your financial statement."

Before I leave, I tell Sharon, "I created a checklist to speed up the chances of helping you. If you and your key people would fill these out and fax or mail them to my attention I will add this to my analysis. Let's meet again in two weeks to see if it makes sense to work together." We set up a date and I head back for my office.

The Gap Analysis

Back at my office the first things I review are See Construction's financial statements. Their statements give clues as to the health of the business.

The first item is sales, which had grown by only 5% per year on average for the last three years. Calculating inflation at 3% left real growth at about 2%. Next I review costs. I notice the statement lists the next few items as "cost of goods." I make a note to question why their accountant doesn't have a more detailed variable cost section.

Next comes gross profit. I get out my copy of the current Robert Morris Report to compare See Construction's gross profit, expenses, net profit, cash flow, and a variety of ratios to similar businesses across the country. When I finish with this form, I review the results. I note that sales need to increase and variable costs need new chart of accounts codes to teach job costs better. Several expense items are off and net profit is off by 5 to 8%. The bottom line is that See Construction is achieving far less than it could be. With total sales of $6,000,000, they are letting approximately $300,000 fall through the cracks.

It's now Wednesday and the checklists I left are coming through the fax. I begin to review each of the forms.

I then write the balance of my report for See Construction based on the completed checklists. It is evident that See Construction does not have most of the written Leadership, Management, Marketing, Sales, Financial and Operations processes necessary for them to close the gaps on their financial statement.

I write that sales are not increasing because there is no marketing plan, no advertising or prospecting process, no sales process, and the CEO is not receiving any of the critical indicating reports necessary to see where the gaps are and correct them.

The company's costs are out of control because there aren't enough leadership and management processes in place to recruit, select, assess, retain, and reward people. Employees aren't accountable and measured because they have no written job descriptions and, no formal meetings, and no skills training. Furthermore, most managers don't receive P&Ls, and the few that do don't really understand how to effect them.

I complete my report for See Construction and call them for an appointment for the following Wednesday. I request they include their key managers in the meeting: those who completed the checklist so I can present my findings in an interactive environment.

I arrive at See Construction Company about five minutes to nine for our nine o'clock meeting and am immediately shown to the conference room area. Sharon and Bill introduce me to each manager, and we all sit down. I give them a brief explanation of my background, the purpose of the meeting, and explain that this is to be an open and informal discussion.

I pass out the reports and begin to cover the highlights of each section. Heads begin to nod, and people start to get motivated when they realize that just about every problem the company and managers are experiencing is caused by the lack of effective processes. I can tell by their questions that these are good, hardworking people who can achieve much more if only the owner and key managers would establish processes. This, then, is the moment of truth. What decision will they make? I can't make them do it; I can only encourage them with the facts and my thirty years experience.

The questions begin to come at me. "How long will this take?" "How much does it cost?" I have developed a form to help them answer these questions based on *their* assessment of costs rather than mine.

We begin with sales. "In order to determine the true costs, don't we first have to determine the cost of the gap?" I ask them. "If you want sales to increase at say 15% a year and they're currently at 5%, then the gap is 10%. Is that right?" They nod yes. "If your sales are at $6,000,000, the 15% goal would be $6,900,000 next year, versus your 5% trend of $6,300,000. So that makes the gap $600,000–the difference between where you should be versus where you are.

"If your gross profit should be 40% according to our Robert Morris Study, then 40% multiplied by $600,000 is $240,000 of lost opportunity. Of course this is just for one year. If you multiply that by five or ten years, you're talking about a lot of money lost, maybe as much as $2,400,000. I believe if you have a dedicated team of people, including the owner, managers, and salespeople, it will take us about three to nine months to develop an effective, written strategic marketing plan, an advertising strategy, and a selling process that will begin to close the sales gap. It's been my experience that sales gains could come much quicker, because in mapping of each process some sales improvements will begin to happen. The only conditions are your industry trend and capacity to produce and deliver those sales.

"I would calculate a training cost of approximately $2,000 a month for everything you will need. This includes all the training materials, forms, processes, and reports. We have created templates where you fill in the blanks and customize each process for your business. This speeds up the whole process and guarantees a comprehensive documented process to increase sales. I would recommend a highly experienced coach and trainer who has written successful plans, created proven marketing and advertising strategies, and has actually sold millions of dollars in products and services to take you through the total process. We have packaged this training into a total cost of approximately $20,000 - $30,000 and then divided it into a monthly retainer of $2,000 to $4,000 per month, depending on how many people are involved, how fast they learn, and how they implement the new skills.

"So for your return on training investment, we will target a gross profit increase of somewhere between $100,000 and $300,000. We will target a return on investment of somewhere between 100% and 300% during the first eighteen months, depending on the conditions we agree on." We continue discussing the points as a group until we agree on what needs to be done to close each gap, the planned result, the people involved, and the time to do it.

The numbers look exciting but possibly unrealistic for the first year, so we modify them slightly. However, the facts are very clear. They need the processes. They need the trained experienced coach. And the cost versus the return is better than anyone expects.

Based on that meeting, I develop a proposal including the processes we will help develop, the training we will give, and the way we will measure the end result. This process took place in December of 1995. By 1996, See Construction's sales were growing at 20% a year. They added ten employees. Their gross profit went from 32% to 41%. Their net profit went from 5% to 15%. And to top it all off, they were chosen as entrepreneur of the year in their local area.

But that's not the end of the story. Not only did they begin to make more money than they ever dreamed of, but their problems were reduced, leaving time for the owners and top management group to focus on the next opportunity, including new products, new services, new markets, new channels, and even a possible acquisition.

The Synergy Factor is Your Process for Success

The feelings I receive from seeing companies like See Construction improve is the reason why I wrote this book. I want to encourage others to do the same. But the biggest objection to processes training is that it represents a substantial change from the way things have been done in the past. Companies are in no hurry to rock the boat, especially if it means taking time or spending money on training. If you catch yourself questioning the importance of training people to document proven processes that will increase predictable results, you're headed for trouble.

Face it, the customer doesn't care how you get the work done or how you make a profit. And the competition isn't going to wait while you figure it out. As a business owner or key manager, you need to develop and implement the proven processes that will help you create the business of your dreams. If you don't, your competition will, and that will most definitely wreak havoc on your business model.

Chapter Ten

Use The Synergy Factor to Ride the Wave to Explosive Cash Flow and Financial Freedom in Any Business

"Genius is the ability to reduce the complicated to the simple."
- *C.W. Ceram*

Think of a business as a Great Lake. The lake is constantly changing. At times it is calm, orderly, and peaceful. At other times, it is chaotic with waves thrashing in every direction. If you were to observe the Great Lake from the shore, however, you would see it from a special perspective. Random and seemingly chaotic movements become organized as a procession of waves comes to shore. Sometimes the waves are small and gentle, while other times they are huge and thrashing. Sail surfers love these conditions. They know how to ride these waves over and over again.

A business, like the Great Lake, also constantly changes. Sometimes it's up; sometimes it's down. It is entangled by a myriad of social, economic, and competitive forces. Like the Great Lake, the business' up and down movements appear to be random. But they are not. Business goes up and down in a distinct pattern of waves. When you have scorecards in place, you can track these highs and lows in order to make out the pattern.

Now is the time to examine the current processes you have in place, if any, and either enhance them or create new ones. To get a better idea of your business' unique need, go through the following checklists and honestly answer each question as it pertains to your business.

Leadership and Management Team Checklist

For each question, answer Yes or No.

1. Have I written out what I want personally in the next three to five years in terms of income and wealth accumulation?

2. Do we have a three to five year strategic plan for sales, profits, cash flow, and stock valuation?

3. Do we have a documented organizational chart for now and for three to five years from now?

4. Do we have job descriptions that include standards for every employee?

5. Have we selected a key management team?

6. Has our management team been trained in mentoring, process mapping and facilitation skills?

7. Do we have effective recruiting, selection, assessment, training, retaining and termination processes?

8. Do we have formal meetings with everyone on a regularly scheduled basis?

9. Do our employees look to the management team for guidance and training?

10. Do we offer effective incentives to keep our people motivated and loyal?

If you answered no to any of the above questions, it's time to enhance or create a leadership and management process that will work for your company.

Marketing, Advertising, and Sales Checklist

For each question, answer Yes or No.

1. Do we have a current effective and written strategic marketing plan?

2. Does our strategic marketing plan include a strategy for each market segment and product or service to achieve our three to five year plan?

3. Have we determined our customers' psychographics, and how they make buying decisions?

4. Have we developed customer demographics that include where they are, what they earn, how old they are, and other valuable personal information?

5. Have we determined our targeted SIC codes, sales ranges, or number of employees?

6. Have we developed a unique advertising message proven to attract customers?

7. Have we developed an advertising and public relations strategy that gets sales people all the leads they need to be productive?

8. Have we developed a quantified selling process map that ensures sales people will be successful if they follow it?

9. Do we receive weekly or monthly reports showing number of leads generated, number of appointments, number of presentations, and number of sales made?

10. Does each member of our sales team know what is expected and how to reach the stated sales goals?

If you answered no to any of the above questions, it's time to enhance or create a sales and marketing process that will work for your company.

Operations Checklist

For each question, answer Yes or No.

1. Do we have a work flow diagram?

2. Is each critical process documented and standardized?

3. Do we have a capacity process?

4. Do we have an accurate sales forecasting process?

5. Do we have a profit analysis process for each job?

6. Do we have skills tests for pre-employment and ongoing training assessments?

7. Do we have documented input and output processes that are measured regularly?

8. Do we have all the production processes in place necessary to get work done on time and on budget?

9. Are we tracking and correcting redos and errors and making changes to stop them from reoccurring?

10. Are the costs, speed, and quality where they need to be?

If you answered no to any of the above questions, it's time to enhance or create an operations process that will work for your company.

Financial Checklist

For each question, answer Yes or No.

1. Have we reviewed the chart of accounts recently for accuracy?

2. Are we receiving monthly accurate financial statements before the 10th of the following month?

3. Do we have budget and variance reports?

4. Do all managers receive profit reports and understand how to take action to change these variables as they occur?

5. Do we have a project profit planning process?

6. Do we have a process that measures each employee's contribution and productivity?

7. Do we have an inventory control process?

8. Do we calculate at least five critical ratios monthly such as ROI, ROS, etc?

9. Do we have a cash plan and budget?

10. Do we have a stock value increasing strategy?

11. Are we 100% satisfied with our financial strategy and processes?

If you answered no to any of the above questions, it's time to enhance or create a financial process that will work for your company.

Ride the Wave of The Synergy Factor

By teaching managers and teams how to develop realistic goals, we can create processes that will achieve those goals and then measure the result of each process, quarterly, monthly, weekly, and daily. By using the data from the included checklists, you can determine which processes need to be developed and how to measure their results.

Always remember that all successfully growing companies that have lasted 20 years or more have the following principles in common:

1. They developed a business model that works.

2. They spent significant time developing and documenting all the critical processes necessary to run the business profitably.

3. They budgeted the time and money necessary to educate the workforce to help them improve in their jobs.

4. They developed a set of core principles/values that have never changed.

5. They developed a process of continuous change to stay in adjustment with the market's ever-changing needs.

6. They followed the 80/20 rule—that 80% of your business will come from 20% of your client base, etc.

7. They focused on putting people first by testing ability, personality and effort.

8. They focused on a meaningful purpose.

9. They focused on profits and cash flow.

10. They had a vision for a better way—the skill to create a strategic plan while at the same time keeping the business moving today.

Where Do We Go From Here?

Discovering where the most serious gaps exist is the first step to developing a solution. The next step is to think creatively in order to meet your goal. This creative thinking is possibly the single most important thing an owner, manager, or technician should know.

Napoleon Hill was a highly successful reporter. He wrote about successful business people and preached that how you thought about your business often resulted in the difference between success and a lack of it.

For me, this is rule number one: You must always protect yourself from focusing on problems and the resulting feelings of despair or helplessness. Instead, ask yourself, "How can I achieve the positive results I desire? How can I get it right?" This is particularly critical if you have a history of thinking negatively or have too many negative influences around you.

The hardest lesson to learn is that you're not going to be right all of the time. And if you don't quickly begin to focus on persistence and new knowledge of a better way of doing things, sooner or later you'll suffer some very large losses. I've known several highly intelligent, educated men and women who were wiped out because they weren't open to the truth of what they were and weren't doing. Brains, experience, ego, stubbornness, and pride are deadly substitutes for having and following sound strategic and quantification processes.

The problem is that most owners and managers always have an intention of solving a problem, increasing sales, or reducing costs when they make a decision. But when they find out they made the wrong decision, they usually wait too long to change and therefore take a bigger loss long term. They find it difficult to admit they were wrong. They'd rather work harder and longer and hope things turn out right.

To make matters worse, when they go back and try to correct the situation, half the time customers and employees are negative or leave. Then they're really upset. They conclude that either the customer or employees were wrong.

How you think about a situation is critical. Historically this is where most business people go wrong and get confused.

Consider the following questions: Did you think about your goals last year? Did you fail to achieve all of them? If you failed to achieve them, were you upset because you wasted your time on goal setting? Will you refuse to set goals this year?

If these thoughts lead you to question why you set goals in the first place, especially if you know you'll fail to achieve them, then it's time to stop and think about this: You set goals because you want a better life, more happiness, more money, and more success. That's all you do when you set goals. You think about what you need to have a better life and what you need to do to get a better result.

How do you define thinking to get a better result? You must begin to raise your awareness of how you think every day. It took me two or three years to acquire the habit of creative thinking. I started each week brainstorming on ways to improve, scheduling time for thinking and writing, feeding my desire, and being persistent in my efforts to achieve what I wanted.

Make this habit yours, and as the years go by, you will get better and better in your thinking process and your problems will drop significantly. You'll find that your failures will be offset by much larger gains from your successes.

Most people would agree that spending time getting an education is a sound decision. They don't think of it as a waste of time because they have hopes that learning will pay off in future success. Why should success in business be any different?

Anything worth succeeding at takes time to learn. Professional craftsmen aren't made in a couple of weeks and neither are successful managers or owners. The only difference between the successful person and the unsuccessful person is determination and persistence.

Becoming a creative thinker takes time. During the process, I have lost jobs, and I have lost money. I have lost customers, and I have lost relationships. But I found a better job. I made more money. I gained new customers. And I improved relationships all to a much higher level than I ever dreamed possible. I've often thought, "What would have happened if I had gotten discouraged and quit because I didn't immediately get the results I really wanted?"

The tricky part is getting rid of the emotions attached to the concept of spending quality time thinking creatively. But the fact is that you must take the time to think about how to motivate people, how to make more profits, how to increase sales faster, how to cut costs, and how to increase productivity. It doesn't feel comfortable to most people to take hours every week or even several days a month and dedicate them to creative thinking. Why is this? Because we feel as if we're not really working, as if we don't have the time to spare. Our emotions take over. We try to defend our original decision to get to work, to answer that phone, and justify not spending time creatively thinking about how to run the business better.

Why is creative thinking the single most important thing an owner or manager should know? Take a moment to consider what would happen if you and your people began to focus blocks of time on creative ways to avoid problems, to prevent rework, to sell more, and to increase profits. Isn't it possible you would begin to see a huge change for the better?

The bottom line is you need to make the decision to schedule time to think about creative ways to improve in order to create lasting change for the better. It takes real commitment, persistence, and desire to make it happen. Otherwise, at the least hint of failure or stress, you will revert back to your old ways.

Think Creatively About Your Synergy

One of the most difficult questions managers and owners ask has to do with predicting whether a synergistic approach will increase performance enough over time to more than pay for the resources invested. One way to help in making this decision is to estimate the cost of not having synergy. If you can develop a specific result that can be measured versus a current condition, you should be able to better predict a meaningful improvement in results versus cost to develop.

Some techniques you must include are:

1. Clearly establish measurable and meaningful improvements.

2. Match the right people to the right process, attitude, and knowledge.

3. Allow adequate time for training and development.

4. Encourage open and honest communications.

5. Give people the authority to act—no red tape.

6. Avoid over optimistic expectations.

7. Create realistic schedules for testing outcomes.

8. Establish realistic cost versus results calculations.

The intangible cost of not acting to meet future needs must be considered as well as the tangible costs of proceeding. In today's rapidly changing business world, a failure to invest in process or product improvements gives competitors who do the opportunity to take away market share. Additionally, because many issues are uncontrollable, such as interest rates, business cycles, and industry trends, a failure to invest in process improvement now may put a business so far behind that it simply can't afford to catch up, as its financial need is beyond its ability to acquire the money to fund it.

For example, if sales, marketing, and advertising processes are not improved and sales continue to be unstable month after month, there will eventually not be the money or resources to continue. If the financial processes are not improved, at some point there will not be enough profit to make the business worth pursuing. If the operations processes are not improved, employee motivation will decline to a point when you begin to ask, "Why did I ever get into this business? I hate even going in to work."

Finally, a failure to invest in process driven teams leads to a business being totally dependent on the owner and a few key managers to continually put out fires, work more hours, and worry about how they will continue to support an ever increasing overhead, with more stress and no way out.

Sometimes a company can get lucky. By lucky I mean a company has one or more big customers that keep sales growing, a great old product or service, or a few key employees the owners can count on. Sometimes a company can be lucky for a long period of time. But do you ever wonder what will happen when the luck runs out?

Without proven effective processes, trained teams, and profit you put yourself at high risk of failure when that big account goes away, or that key employee is no longer there, or your product or service can't compete. Do you look forward with a sense of confidence this year that you will grow profits? Is that sense just a hunch? Can you look three to five years into the future to a time that you will be free from the same stress and worry you have had in the past?

What is the cost of not having effective recruiting and marketing processes? What is the cost of not having a cash flow planning process? Additionally, what is it costing you right now? What are the cost consequences of procrastination, of putting it off with excuses like "we don't have the time" or "we can't afford it"?

Ultimately, you and your key managers are responsible for every business decision and the resulting consequences, whether good or bad. From this point on there are no excuses. So if you're done with excuses and have decided to reach for your real potential, then you can begin now to close every gap and gain the profits and productivity you desire.

When you begin to spend time creatively thinking and developing the necessary teams and processes to run your business, you'll begin to reach new levels of success. This is an evolutionary process, and by beginning with a few hours that expands over time, you'll come to a point where the synergy factor kicks in and speeds up the process to its conclusion.

Conclusion

Holt Marketing and Management Services found that any business can succeed if they will take the time to select the right people, not only for the job but to fit within the culture of that business.

They must develop a strategic plan that identifies what the customer prefers and how to deliver that as a company. Then select the right people, and train them in the processes that delivers that unique result. Cross functional teams must develop the processes to keep the business growing in the key functional areas of leadership, operations, marketing and finance. Keep score of important indicators and change whatever is necessary to stay ahead of the competition.

"The Lord said: now these people are united, all speaking the language. This is only the beginning of what they will do. They will be able to do anything they want."
                                              Genesis 11:1 - 11:6

I wish you luck and prosperity in all your business endeavors.

Afterward

So Now What Can You Do?

Now that you want to get started... Now that you want to move up to the next level of success... You should stop and make an assessment of where you are versus where you want to be. The gaps will tell you exactly what needs to be done to get to your next level, whatever that may be.

What you'll discover is that the gap is always created by the absence of trained people, the right processes or the right strategy.

Since I started in 1985, we have coached and trained over 200 businesses owners on how to create the right strategy, select and train the right people and develop the processes that all but guarantee success.

We would like to do the same for you by conducting a Gap Analysis. Holt Marketing & Management's Gap Analysis System provides you with a crystal clear understanding of the exciting opportunities available to you.

To move forward simply complete the form at the back of this book or call us at **1.800.698.2449**

After Andrew Carnegie had started, built and sold United States Steel for over $900,000,000 in cash in 1900 (making him the richest man on Earth) he was asked; "How can you tell which people will succeed in business?" Mr. Carnegie replied; "As I grow older, I pay less attention to what men say. I just watch what they really do."

Let's get going!
- Gary Holt

If you would like more information or if you would like to be contacted please complete the form below and check the areas you are interested in. There is no cost or obligation.

For more information on:
- ❏ Leadership & Management Skills
- ❏ Strategic Marketing and Branding
- ❏ Recruiting/Retaining Quality People
- ❏ Increasing Sales and Cash Flow
- ❏ Personality and Ability Testing
- ❏ Business Gap Analysis
- ❏ Team Development
- ❏ Process Mapping
- ❏ Using Scorecards
- ❏ Bonus Incentives
- ❏ Management Surveys
- ❏ Leadership and Goal Setting
- ❏ Other_____

Contact name: _____

Business Name: _____

Address_____

City_____ State_____ Zip_____-_____

Phone Number_____ Fax Number_____

FAX
989.791.2473
VISIT us at:
www.marketingholt.com

CALL
800.698.2449
EMAIL us at:
garyh@marketingholt.com

MAIL:
3075 Boardwalk
Saginaw, MI 48603

About the Author

Throughout his 35 years in business, Gary A. Holt has received numerous awards as well as recognition as an innovative leader in Marketing and Management. Born in 1941, he grew up in East Detroit, Michigan where he began his extensive background in executive positions with companies like: J.L. Hudson's, Chrysler, Howmett, Grinnells, Meier Brass and S&H Stores.

In 1985 Gary started his first company called American Advertising with his wife, and was on the start-up team of Signtec (a high-tech sign company). In 1990, Gary began Holt Marketing Services, Inc., a consulting, training and full service advertising agency based in Saginaw, Michigan to help companies discover and harness the power of their "unique promise" and develop cross functional management teams.

Gary's specialty is improving the profits through Strategic Planning, Tracking Systems, Process Mapping, and Sales Training. In fifteen years he has helped over 200 companies achieve their true potential. To date, over a thousand business owners, managers and sales people have benefited from working with Gary and learning the fundamental processes needed to make any business achieve success.

He has received his certification in strategic Planning and Process Mapping at Michigan State University, and is certified as an E-Myth conultant.